T0247680

BRUCE SPRINGSTEEN

50 YEARS OF ROCK 'N' ROLL

whitestar°

CONTENTS

EVERYTHING ENDS WITH A SONG

FOREWORD by Leonardo Colombati

In his memoir, *My Past and Thoughts,* Aleksandr Herzen writes: "I do not know why the memories of first love are given such precedence over the memories of youthful friendship... Bless your fate if you have had youth (merely being young is not enough for this), and bless it doubly if you had a friend then." It's true: in the end, your first kiss is always a bit random, isn't it? While your first friend is a much more conscious decision, it's the end of loneliness, the relief of feeling—finally—anything but singular. If your adolescence also then fell between the 40 years that spanned from "That's All Right (Mama)" to "Smells Like Teen Spirit" and you want to bless your fate three times, do it, if in your adolescence you came across artists like Elvis Presley and Kurt Cobain, and that whole lineup of sorcerers who in some weird way whispered, at least once, "Give me three minutes, just three minutes of your time and I'll change your life" into your young, impressionable ear. I'm talking about Chuck Berry and Ray Charles, Bob Dylan and Paul Simon, Lennon & McCartney and Jagger & Richards, Lou Reed and Jimi Hendrix, Janis Joplin and Stevie Wonder, Tom Waits and Patti Smith, Joni Mitchell and Jackson Browne, Joe Strummer and Bob Marley, Prince and Kate Bush, Morrissey and Michael Stipe...

Not to mention Bruce Springsteen.

If you came across Bruce Springsteen—the musical equivalent of Winston Churchill, John Wayne, and Albert Schweitzer—well, you were lucky. Or you have great musical instincts. Because with Springsteen, not only in three minutes did you learn more than what you parroted at school, but perhaps you even caught his live show, and in those three hours (which every so often even reach four) you've undoubtedly had the furtive but profound impression that, as Louis Armstrong and Sam Cooke (talk about magic) once sang, it's a wonderful world, despite climate change, social injustice, and the insipid fluff by Ed Sheeran.

Is rock dead? Yes. But it was wonderful while it lasted. For 40 years, rock music not only made us whistle in the shower or croon serenades below a window, but it used songs as a vehicle with which to tell a story, protest, and even make us think! And in that sense, I truly can't think of a greater writer than Bruce Springsteen. Who has made me sweat more below a stage than Bruce Springsteen? From him, I learned that if you modify a '69 Chevy with a 396 engine, all the dudes in LA will eat your dust; that when going down Broadway either you walk tall or you don't walk at all; that you shouldn't EVER mix Tanqueray and wine (just look what happened to Johnny 99); that at the back of every bar there's always a girl who doesn't look TOO married; that it isn't worth looking for a job with the Johnstown Company; and that in Reno, a prostitute charges "two hundred dollars straight in, two-fifty up the ass."

When I was fourteen, I bought a book by Ernesto Assante titled *Il Rock and Altre Storie (Rock and Other Stories)*. I don't know any other genre of music, literature, or film with as many tales to tell as rock, each one so different from the next. What do Aretha Franklin and Amy Winehouse, Johnny Cash and Boy George, Ian Curtis and Michael Jackson have in common? In the meantime, feast your eyes on the story that unravels upon the pages that follow, because this is one of those tales that has a bit of everything: Homer and *West Side Story*, Marlon Brando and Roy Orbison, Steinbeck and *The Searchers*, Nebraska and Vietnam, *Happy Days* and *The Sopranos*, Elvis and Bob Dylan, wrecked Buicks and a pink Cadillac, pimps and serial killers, deserted highways and packed stadiums, gangsters blowing each other up in Philly and girls on the hood of a car drinking warm beer in the soft summer rain. And remember: don't feel too bad if it ends up being a story that stays with you, more so than most of the "serious" books you've read. Because, as that witty genius Beaumarchais realized 250 years ago, *tout finit par des chansons*. Everything ends with a song.

"Rock doesn't mean just one thing, because every great culture reflects many human conditions, which are always different. We all try to make sense of a world that's otherwise incomprehensible. When you're young, you try to do so by how you dress or how you cut your hair. And by listening to rock 'n' roll. At 14 or 15 years old, it gives you structure, but it works at 48, 49, or 50 years old all the same. Rock is music that presents complicated ideas in a simple way; it speaks directly to the heart and soul; it's a small yet powerful tool. It tries to shape the

ROCK DOESN'T MEAN JUST ONE THING, BECAUSE EVERY GREAT CULTURE REFLECTS MANY HUMAN CONDITIONS

world: Elvis, Dylan, Public Enemy, the Sex Pistols, they did it with great music. Rock appeared in the 1950s to offer a place to go, culturally and spiritually, to young people who rejected the traditional world, which had no place for them. I think it's still that way today. And me? I'm just a prisoner of rock 'n' roll. . . .

5 *A portrait of Bruce Springsteen at the start of his career, taken for a marketing campaign.*

8 *Springsteen during one of the Springsteen on Broadway concerts at the St. James Theatre in New York City, June 26, 2021.*

Springsteen is rock 'n' roll, something elusive yet substantial, something that enlivens life and which life itself enlivens. Sex, sweat, tears, passion, love, energy, rebellion, hope. But Bruce—born Frederick Joseph Springsteen on September 23, 1949 in Freehold, New Jersey—isn't just the last great hero of rock 'n' roll. He's much more: he's the most recent heir to great literary

His performances aren't just concerts, but a celebration of life.

traditions that start with the primitivism of the pioneers, continue on through Walt Whitman, Ralph Waldo Emerson, Mark Twain, and the Beat Generation to reach today, a scion in a line of poets who have sung of wide-open fields and interior spaces, who have mixed small roads and large highways, who have celebrated the frontier spirit and the eternal youth of the United States of America without being blinded by its lights. He is also the last great singer of freedom, the same freedom that so many folk, rock, and pop songs have celebrated and still celebrate, but which he embodies with strength and emotion.

11 *The Boss and his guitar, during a concert in Providence, Rhode Island on January 24, 1985.*

12-13 *Two moments from the Oakland, California concert that was part of the Born in the U.S.A. tour, 1984.*

14-15 *Springsteen backstage at Madison Square Garden in 2018.*

He's also leader of the masses, a messiah, "a long-awaited arrival, the star of incredible transformation," the savior of our souls through music, with the instrument of songs, with the power of sound, with the electricity of a guitar. Those who have seen him in concert know this to be true, that his performances aren't just "shows," but a secular mass in which the collective dream of a better, more just life for all suddenly seems within reach, a celebration of the life that pushes a community to rise up, for about four hours, to a state of grace that is impossible to reach otherwise. And even if the catharsis, the "magic rite of purification, understood as cleansing the body and the soul of all contamination" doesn't happen, the audience has still seen a show with uncontrollable energy, a sort of vivacity and force that others don't offer. And a kind of "truth" that others don't possess. The authenticity of his concerts is the true seal of the pact between him and the audience, the place where his music becomes truly "real," as if his songs had been written just to be sung in that precise moment, in that exact place, in the magic space that he creates during a concert, where time stands still, a place in which everyone is suspended in a shared, collective dimension that's unrepeatable otherwise. And that is exactly what we'll try to recount in this story, one that has been told a thousand times before and which will be told a thousand times again in the years to come. The story of a boy who left the heartland where he grew up to conquer the heart of the world, to share it with others, to sing about it at the top of his lungs, to encapsulate it in a "one, two, three, four," and to tie it to his and ours with the string of a guitar.

ROCK 'N' ROLL HAS MANY SOULS
AND MANY LIVES. BRUCE SPRINGSTEEN
TRULY EMBODIES THEM ALL.

1

1949–1973
GREETINGS FROM
ASBURY PARK

AN AUTOMOBILE,
AN ELECTRIC GUITAR,
AND BIG DREAMS

Bruce Springsteen grew up in the small town of Freehold, New Jersey, 38 miles (60 km) from Manhattan, population 35,000 at the last census: much, much smaller than when the Springsteen and Zerilli families moved there. So small that, as Springsteen noted in his autobiography, the first mass and the first funeral of the city were held in the living room of his house, at 87 Randolph Street. On the streets of Freehold, Springsteen grew up, he decided which limits he wanted to overcome, he forged friendships, some of which were extremely long-lasting, he learned the logic of the street, of the streets, the big ones that lead elsewhere and the small ones that go nowhere, the side streets which, unseen, get you to downtown anyway, and the trails that are meant to be walked alone. An Irish father and an Italian mother, a poor family, but not too poor. Springsteen was

HE GREW UP ON THE STREETS OF FREEHOLD,
DARK SIDE STREETS
AND LONG, WIDE-OPEN HIGHWAYS

anything but a "boss" as a child. Or rather, at his grandparents' house, he was a "boss" from a young age: spoiled, free, and pampered. But at home with his parents, his dad, Douglas Springsteen, was in charge and he marched to an entirely different tune. "I was not my father's favorite citizen," Springsteen explains in his autobiography. "I was 'soft.' And he hated 'soft.' Of course, he'd been brought up 'soft.' A mama's boy, just like me." But little Bruce had a place he could escape to, where he'd find comfort, freedom, and warmth: the house of his paternal grandparents, the Irish branch of the family, which almost never intermingled with the Italian side, even if they lived just a few blocks away from each other. Their influence on him was enormous and, in that house, he was a 'little king' who did what he wanted when he wanted to; he was given free rein. It was only when the scepter was taken from him, starting from the first day of school, that everything changed.

But it wasn't his family, neighborhood, friends, or even the radio or music in the air. It was the Catholic school he attended, more precisely St. Rose of Lima in Freehold, his hometown, to have the greatest influence on his music. It was a school run by nuns, the classic vessel for military-like rules camouflaged as religious rigor, catechism followed to a T, religious services at set times, host wafers by the pound, ranks to keep, orders and hierarchy, for the nuns and the students alike. It was a barracks in which guns were replaced by sacred hymns, livery replaced by school uniforms, and prayers instead of target practice. Everything else was exactly the same.

Young Bruce Springsteen wasn't at ease there, in the most authoritarian place that a child could spend time. Or perhaps, looked at a different way, it was the easiest place for his true nature to come through. Because it was there that his rejection of authority, his passion for rebellion and breaking out of the box, was cemented.

He never became a fan of studying throughout his academic life (a life stripped to the bone, let's be clear), and he always had a bone to pick with the nuns in particular. Yet, perhaps thanks to the power that the fear of God can have over a child, he was a believer, he was Catholic. His faith was so strong that he even later developed a range of problems and issues relating to his first sexual experiences. He believed in God, in the Holy Spirit, in the Virgin Mary and the Baby Jesus. "In Catholicism, there existed the poetry, danger and darkness that reflected my imagination and my inner self," he writes in his autobiography. "I found a land of great and harsh beauty, of fantastic stories, of unimaginable punishment and infinite reward. It was a glorious and pathetic place I was either shaped for or fit right into. It has walked alongside me as a waking dream my entire life. So as a young adult, I tried to make sense of it. I tried to meet its challenge for the very reasons that there *are* souls to lose and a kingdom of love to be gained." In short, he was young, but he already had that which those who have them love to call 'ironclad values.' The thing he never believed in was the imposition of authority. And he never would believe in it. He never believed in it to the point that it shaped an entire life dedicated to singing about the joy of escaping the grasp of those structures.

He wasn't the coolest kid at school. But he was attentive, vivacious, and curious.

He wasn't the coolest kid at school or the most outgoing, but he was attentive; he observed, watched, understood, and learned about the world around him. But influence is one thing, and an epiphany is another. The single moment in which everything changed, the flash of what his future could be, as Bruce Springsteen, happened at seven years old, when he saw Elvis Presley play on the Ed Sullivan Show. The show was a must-watch for anyone who listened to or was interested in a certain type of music, performances, irony and American-style spectacle. Sullivan presented musicians riding the rock wave, so seeing someone perform on TV was nothing new. What was new, was seeing Elvis. It was September 9, 1956, and the performance (the first of the three between 1956 and 1957) on one of the most popular television programs in America caught he attention of 82% of the television viewing audience. Eight out of ten spectators in the U.S. were watching. "The revolution HAS been televised," Springsteen himself said years later, riffing on Gil Scott-Heron, and then adding that the message broadcast through that performance was "if you were born in America, that freedom and entertainment were your birthright." Elvis was the spark, the clear, shining vision that a different life was possible, one that didn't take place at the intersection of Randolph and McLean, the two streets that were at the heart of young Bruce's universe. Elvis said loud and clear that his small, closed, unchangeable world was over, done for, a world to forget about. That there was more out there, that dreams can come true and desires can become reality. That there's rock 'n' roll, and nothing else matters.

Elvis was so crucial to the idea of becoming a musician that, almost thirty years after that night, Springsteen allegedly broke into his home. Not only was he no longer a child (he was thirty-six years old), but at the time of the event, *Born to Run* was already out. In other words, he was already famous—so famous that he had graced the cover of *Newsweek*. The occasion came about almost by accident, though seizing it was perhaps less so. While in Memphis in 1975, Springsteen was riding in a taxi at night with Steve Van Zandt, in search of somewhere to eat. The taxi driver suggested a place not far from Elvis's house. Those words—Elvis's house—the fact that there was even a vague possibility of being near the King's home, were all it took for his imagination to run wild. He told the cab driver to take him straight there. The gate that broke up the high walls of the estate was closed, but he could see that the lights were on, off in the distance. The two passengers started planning their break-in, while the driver, who at that point was a full part of the plot, warned them: "There are dogs. Big dogs." The most famous, most talked-about emerging musician in America thus climbed the wall surrounding the property and ran as fast as he could, escaping from imaginary dogs up to the front door, like any fan in the throes of an illogical frenzy. The security guard stopped him just before he could knock. Elvis wasn't home, he was in Lake Tahoe. "Can you tell him Bruce Springsteen stopped by? I'm on the cover of *Newsweek*." "OK, I'll let him know." End of the story. Still today, fans do the same thing to him, hopping over his fence and showing up in his house, trying to meet him and rubbing the fact that he once did the same to Elvis in his face.

1956

A GUITAR, AT JUST SEVEN YEARS OLD
and Elvis was the key to a world
made of constant discontent

Disdain for the rules of a Catholic education which then became the zeal of an Elvis fanatic. He was sent to the school run by nuns by his father, Dutch-Irish Douglas Springsteen, and mother, Adele Ann (née Zerilli), with Neapolitan, obviously Catholic roots, the pillar that kept the family standing. Douglas battled mental health problems his entire life, which, of course, went undiagnosed at the time. He hopped from one job to the next, blue-collar roles mostly: from bus driver to factory worker. Adele Ann, on the other hand, was the breadwinner of the family with her regular paycheck as a legal secretary. They never were destitute, so it wasn't a matter of going hungry or knowing true poverty, as the origin stories of the most derelict musicians often recount. Instead, they fell squarely in the lower class. Sending him to Catholic school was a big sacrifice that his mother was willing to make, even if Springsteen didn't exactly excel. He was very introverted and remained so at least until graduation. He hated that place and wanted to leave it behind each and every day. His wish was granted, finally, when he was six years old, in 1955, when his father lost yet another job and the family had to find a new place to live, closer to his maternal grandparents, at least until Douglas found the next job in a long line of them, in a county penitentiary. Continuously moving from school to school wasn't ideal for a boy who already was introverted, and young Bruce never truly set down roots at school; it wasn't there that he would forge the crucial ties of his lifetime. However, the long wave of Elvis's television performance led to a clear request: a guitar. A guitar, even if it made no sense. After all, he was just seven years old and his fingers were still too small for the Kent that his mother rented for him. There was no instant gratification, and that instrument did nothing for him. Essentially, it didn't transform him into Elvis. And the boring, repetitive guitar lessons he took clearly didn't make things better. He lasted two weeks, then he gave up and the rented guitar was returned. But before giving it back, he put on a show, the first show of his life, in the back of the house for an audience made up of kids and neighbors. He didn't play the guitar, he didn't know how, but he performed all the moves and struck all the right poses. It was a disaster, of course, but it was a taste. In the years that followed, it took a lot of perseverance and tenacity to keep playing in some way and, in spite of it all, to earn what would become the first in a long series of nicknames and aliases: Billy. That was the term used by locals to refer to people who strummed away on their porches, seated in a rocking chair. Because when Bruce Springsteen played, he played alone.

1963: Springsteen was 14 years old and nothing had changed in his life, until everything changed. His father continued to be a bit cold, his mother supported the family, and he was now in high school. He still had a terrible relationship with his teachers, and he was so introverted that he was seen as a sort of zombie. The thing that brought about real change was the arrival of his first very own electric guitar, with the price

IN 1963, MUSIC CHANGED. NO MORE SINATRA OR ROCK 'N' ROLL, BUT THE BEATLES WITH ALL THEIR VITALITY.

tag of $69 (the equivalent of $580 today), no small expense. "My guitar was as cheap as they came; but compared to the junker I'd been playing, it was a Cadillac," he remembered. It was a yellow Fender, and he still has it today.

The guitar wasn't the only thing to change in 1963. At that time, Springsteen's musical tastes were evolving, he went from the rock 'n' roll and Frank Sinatra of the 1950s (another New Jersey native, like him) to Phil Spector, doo wop and many soul acts coming out of Motown and Stax Records, of course, with their wind-forward sound. It was all very important, but paled in comparison with the moment he saw the Beatles, once again on the Ed Sullivan Show. It was

their famous 1964 performance: "I sat there, heart pounding, waiting for the first real look at my new saviors, waiting to hear the first redemptive notes come peeling off the Rickenbacker, Hofner, and Gibson guitars in their hands."

With the guitar he bought at Caiazzo's Music Store on Center Street, complete with a small amp, came his first bands. They had names like the Rogues, or the later and more important the Castiles, where he played lead guitar and, like his bandmates, brushed his hair into Beatle haircuts. They were the groups of his youth, but they were serious. They played in pizzerias and roller rinks for $35 a night, even earning some level of local fame. Their repertory was made mostly of cover songs, Motown classics, and of course a few tracks from the bands of the British Invasion—the Beatles mainly, but also the Rolling Stones and the Who, or even something a bit out-of-character for a beat band, like *In the Mood* by Glenn Miller. Sure, they had a few songs of their own, but Springsteen didn't write them. Moreover, he certainly couldn't be considered the leader of the band, though without a doubt he experienced music differently than all the others. Well, not quite. There was someone who lived and breathed it just as he did. His name was Steven Van Zandt, and he played in the Shadows and, one night or another, the two became friends, a friendship that has lasted up to today.

25 *Bruce Springsteen at 17 years old, in his high school yearbook.*

In the orbit of the Castiles there was also Gordon Vinyard, a.k.a. Tex, the manager of the band and the person responsible for booking their shows (and the one who gave them their name). Vinyard worked hard and even managed to get them booked for a month straight in Greenwich Village, at Café Wha?. It was 1967, Springsteen was eighteen, and that month spent in New York, far away from Freehold, practically sealed the deal on his failure. It took a miracle (not any effort on his part) to get through it. He hadn't overcome his tendency not to make friends, he didn't go out with others, and, if he wasn't playing music, he was tinkering with cars. So, it was a big surprise to everyone when, the following year (1968), he promptly enrolled at Ocean County College. He didn't seem like the type of guy to keep studying after high school, but college was one of the many ways not to be shipped off to Vietnam. Though, if things were bad in high school, they were even worse in college. He was no longer seen as an introvert, but was catapulted straight to the category of psychopath, a nobody. He lasted a year. Plus, he was the type of guy that had read only two books in his entire life (*The Godfather* by Mario Puzo, and the biography of Bob Dylan), and if he went to the movie theater it was to see Westerns, specifically those by Roy Rogers (as a kid), and then those by Leone and Ford (as an adult).

Inevitably, dropping out of college led to being drafted to the army. It was the life that his father, Douglas, had repeatedly hung over him, threateningly, saying that his loudmouth attitude, long hair, and rebellious character would be quashed once he finally joined the army and was turned into a man. But it was also a time when many of his peers were shipped off and very few came back. More specifically, one of the ones to never come back was Bart Haynes, the first real drummer and serious friend Springsteen had ever played with, who voluntarily enlisted with the Marines and was killed in 1967. They were friends, they were in the Castiles together, and Haynes was the first person from Freehold to die in Vietnam, though certainly not the last. One year later, among the many others who didn't make it back was Walter Chicon, an idol to Springsteen and a local rock star who never recorded an album or went on tour, but who was the best of the best, a rock god in the music scene on the New Jersey

27 *Dress rehearsal for stardom, with long hair in 1968.*

coast. Chicon didn't need to sell records or go on tour to be a rock star through and through; he simply had the right attitude. And he was the first rock star that Springsteen had ever seen. He wanted to be like him, and he carefully soaked up every detail of his performances. To Springsteen, that persona spoke volumes, saying that on the stage you could be sensual, dangerous, natural, and free, that no one could tell you how to live your life. Chicon's being killed in the war was a heavy blow. There was good reason to be terrified of being called to the army, and Springsteen certainly was. When the draft notice came, he ran away, stayed out all night, and the morning after reported to the recruiter's office along with Mad Dog Lopez and another friend, all drafted on the same day, and all of them sent home. His attitude was deemed unsuitable and, together with a head injury from a motorcycle accident at seventeen years old, it saved him. He wasn't to be shipped off. Spared thanks to his rebellious air. He was relieved, but he knew that his father was waiting for him at home. He had disappeared for two days without checking in, and, perhaps more importantly, he had been rejected by the military. When he got home that night, he found his father standing in the kitchen, in the dark. Bruce said: "They didn't take me." His father replied: "That's good." And they never talked about it again.

THE VIETNAM WAR CAME KNOCKING ON HIS FRONT DOOR. BUT HE AND HIS FRIENDS WERE DECLARED UNFIT.

1969 thus came crawling along amid evenings booked by Vinyard (who was the manager of another of Springsteen's groups, the Legends), dropping out of college, avoiding being drafted, the release of *Once Upon a Time in the West* by Sergio Leone and, finally, a life-changing event. The family moved to the West Coast with the youngest daughter, Pam, while Virginia, who was just one year younger than Bruce, had gotten pregnant, then married at eighteen years old, and was living in another city in New Jersey.

Springsteen was nineteen years old, alone, without a dime, without his family and with an uncertain future. He tried to stay in his parents' house with Dani Federici and Vini Lopez as roommates, but they were kicked out by the landlord after just a month. Springsteen packed up the few things he owned into a pickup and took off with a few other members of the band. He left Freehold on a summer night, a story he's recounted many times, sprawled out on a sofa in the back of a pickup truck as it crossed the city to leave town. He recounts that moment as one of pure happiness, while, lying on his back, he watched the trees and stars as they passed by, a time in which he had "a blank page challenging him to write his story" in front of him. It was his "Thunder Road."

When he left Freehold, he discovered he had a blank page before him waiting to be written.

The destination wasn't too far: from Freehold he moved to Asbury Park, about twenty-four minutes on the highway. It's another small city in New Jersey, except that it's on the coast. There he lived on the second floor of a surfboard workshop, the owner of which was his new manager, Carl Virgil West, a.k.a. Tinker.

It goes without saying that his life became one long night out in the local venues. The school introvert started to meet people, and everyone in the local New Jersey music scene became part of his circle of friends, including, of course, those who would become part of the

The groups he played in, founded, left, and broke up were Earth (a power trio) and then Child, which later became Steel Mill. It was at this time that he forged the most important friendships.

Steel Mill already included Danny Federici, Vini Lopez, and Vinnie Roslin. The bars and clubs they played in most often had names like Stone Pony and Upstage. The managers of the latter still perfectly remember what happened the first time Springsteen walked in: he very politely asked for a guitar at the bar, then he started playing the blues. It might sound normal for Springsteen, but actually the music he was putting out with Steel Mill at the time was different, it was very tense rock full of solos (after all, it was the cusp of the 1970s, the years of progressive rock). But in that moment, he was foreshadowing the more classic tones of his career as a solo artist and, again according to the managers of the club, it was clear to everyone there that someone who truly knew how to play had walked in. That's what made him stand out, yet it wasn't innate. It came from experience that was out of scale compared to anyone else. According to Springsteen himself, at that point in his life, he had played in an incredible quantity and variety of places that ranged from fireman festivals to nighttime openings of supermarkets, drive-ins, beach parties, policeman's associations, pizzerias, cafes, and even bowling alleys, trailer parks, and roller rinks. He had played in museums, food banks, gyms, county fairs, theme parks, school dances, and even weddings and bar mitzvahs, without forgetting a few rather unique shows, one in Sing Sing prison and one at the psychiatric hospital of Marlboro. All before turning twenty-three. The fact that he was frustrated, resentful, and jealous of the musicians he heard on the radio was entirely to be expected. He thought he was better than them and he couldn't understand why he hadn't been discovered. New Jersey clearly was to blame, the "armpit of the world." So, he, Tinker West, and Steel Mill decided to head to California for a nice, long tour. They pooled $1,000 and set out on a three-day road trip, arriving for the New Year's Eve concert they were booked to play in Big Sur. They spent three days taking turns behind the wheel of two cars, without stopping, to get there in time: seventy-two hours of non-stop driving!

The two cars that the members of Steel Mill were traveling in lost sight of each other almost immediately, near Nashville, Tennessee, after the first twelve hours of their trip. Springsteen was in the car with Tinker and his dog, but he didn't have a driver's license, and he didn't know how to drive. At a certain point he had to drive anyway so that Tinker could sleep and, to get to the New Year's party on time, he covered 2,175 miles (3,500 km) without ever having driven America's infinite highways before.

It was the first time that Springsteen truly saw the United States of America. All of it.

Unlike the bands he had played with up to that point, Steel Mill was a more organized project. Their live set was original and well thought-out, and when they took to the stage they were a success, they made waves. So much so that they were asked to record their first demo in the studio owned by Bill Graham, the "god" of all Californian rock managers. But it ended there. They were offered "some sort of retainer fee, but nothing that showed any real interest," and their dreams were shattered just as quickly as they had taken shape. In the meantime, the band had changed, and Springsteen was now the leader. He was the one to take charge, to write the songs and, most importantly, the lyrics. He was still green, of course,

and he was trying to do what everyone else was doing, write songs that are catchy and fun to listen to. Moreover, the only listeners they had were concertgoers, the ones at the clubs where they managed to get booked (which were very few, to the extent that their California dream was shattered and the band returned to their home base, New Jersey). But Springsteen was refining his technique, and the joke at the time was that no one else managed to get so many words in a song as he did. He was the band's leader, but he was also its problem member. Continuous disagreements became true arguments, which at times even wound up as fistfights. Two hellish years ended in 1971 with Steel Mill breaking up and another band being founded: Dr. Zoom & the Sonic Boom. Exiled to the new band along with Springsteen were his friends Federici and Lopez, joined on a permanent basis by Steve Van Zandt. They were inseparable.

This time, however, Springsteen had a clear plan in mind. This time, he didn't want the usual group, but a giant band; he wanted to try to find, recruit, and engage as many musicians as possible. The lineups of his groups at the time were flexible, to say the least, with members constantly coming and going. The dream was of an 11-piece mega group with wind instruments and female singers, a sort of swing-band setup but playing rock and soul, with completely original songs. However, if he wasn't able to keep a power trio or a mid-size band together, finding another nine people to get along with was a lost cause. The search for the perfect group was destined to fail and fail again.

31 *Bruce Springsteen in 1978, in his house in Haddonfield, New Jersey.*

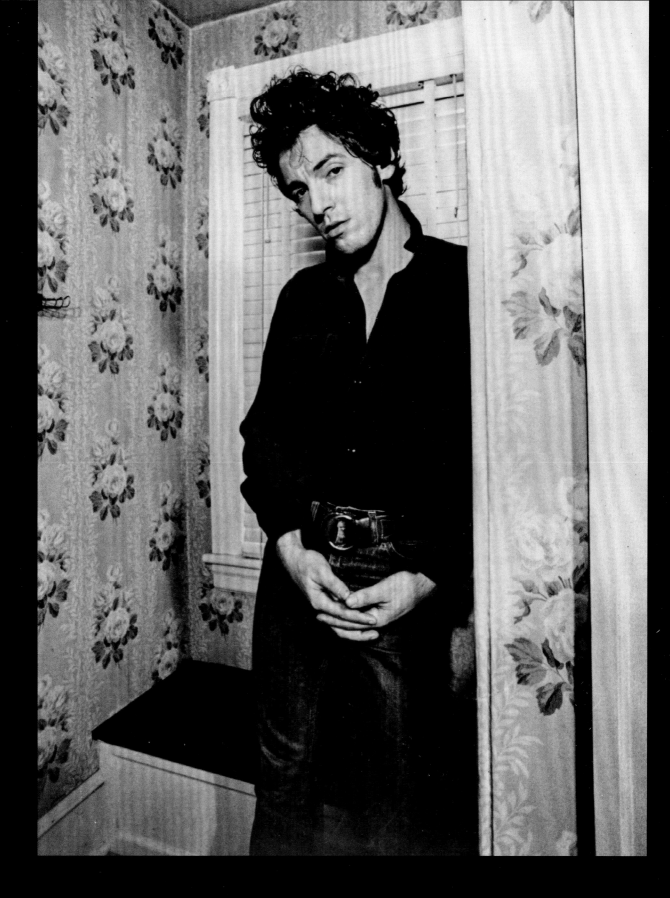

1970

But we've gotten ahead of ourselves. In the meantime, the decade was changing, going from 1969 to 1970. Steel Mill became a relatively famous band in the Asbury Park area, then they rapidly broke up and Springsteen decided to get another band together, with two fundamental arrivals: Gerry Tallent and David Sancious. The idea was for the group to be named after him, the Bruce Springsteen Band, which he considers "one of the smartest decisions of my young life." And why not? After all, he was the front-man, musician, and singer and songwriter of their entire repertoire, which meant doing away with all that was superfluous: "I didn't want to get into any more decision-making squabbles or have any confusion about who set the creative direction of my music," Springsteen remembers in his autobiography. "I wanted the freedom to follow my 'muse' without unnecessary argument." He is Bruce Springsteen, after all. The Boss.

Originally, he was "the Doc," but he soon became "the Boss." There are lots of rumors and legends in that regard, but only one thing is 100% for sure: Springsteen didn't like it, he never has, but he's given in. He loves to say that it comes from the fact that it was always up to him, at the end of the night, to get the money from the owner of the bar or club, and divide it up between his bandmates, who ironically dubbed him "boss." Others tell a different tale. According to them, it all came about in the living room of Steve Van Zandt's

LEADER, MUSICIAN, SINGER IN A BAND. BRUCE, IN SPITE OF HIMSELF, BECAME THE BOSS.

apartment, which was perpetually without heat, on the outskirts of Asbury Park, and by rough, bloody games of Monopoly (with his bandmates, of course, since he's never so much as mentioned any friends outside the world of music), in which Springsteen dominated, forming alliances between one throw of the dice and the next. He would corrupt, grease the wheels and negotiate, applying the maximum power of persuasion to obtain favors or parcels of the most-sought-after properties. His favorite bribes were lollipops and Pepsi, earning him the nickname of Gut Bomb King, then, definitively, *the Boss*.

It's a nickname that, unlike many others that they gave each other, didn't just disappear. It stuck. Instead of abating over time and disappearing, everyone continued to use it, then other people heard it and started to use it too. To rebel and ask them not to was of course useless, so much so that, for at least three years, the Boss (which he really was) dictated that the nickname was to be used within the circle of the band only. Then he decided that the roadies could use it, as could the members of other bands or the friends that, in turn, had a nickname that he himself had given them. It all came crumbling down when, in 1974, a journalist heard a propman call him "Boss" backstage during a concert. That journalist added it to his piece, and the attempts to shake himself of that nickname, or at least contain it, flew out the window. He was and always will be *the Boss*.

Between 1971 and 1972, Bruce Springsteen actually became Bruce Springsteen. Being Bruce Springsteen meant starting a new life, and he did it thinking of Bob Dylan: "Bob pointed true north and served as a beacon to assist you in making your way through the new wilderness America had become." A singer-songwriter, and not just a rocker or soul musician. He wrote different songs, more intimate ones, not just catchy hooks to make the audience go wild. They were personal tales, stories about America, snapshots of what he'd seen and experienced, artistic songs. He turned into a singer-songwriter, dropping the band, playing with nothing and no one but his guitar, a little rock, and a lot of passion. Today, it's easy to see that those shows were already gems, it's all there, even if he's on stage alone, with nothing but his voice, his words, his way of singing them. The authenticity, the pure, simple truth that anyone who listens to him senses and understands, is there too. There's a new Bruce Springsteen, whose metamorphosis has been helped and supported by Mike Appel, his new manager, who truly believes in him, in his potential, in his gift. Appel was a showbiz go-between, a hyperactive person who got so excited about Springsteen that he got him an audition at Columbia Records on May 2 in front of the man who signed countless stars to Columbia, including Billie Holiday, Bessie Smith, and Benny Goodman. The same man who "discovered" Bob Dylan. The audition went so well that Hammond asked Springsteen to play live in front of the other Columbia record execs that night, booking the Gaslight. The following day, at 10:30 am, he called him in to record his first demos, twelve tracks. Clive Davis, the head of Columbia, listened to them and decided to sign Springsteen, giving him his first record deal on June 9. Springsteen's purebred talent was confirmed on September 30, 1972 by John Hammond himself, interviewed by *Record World:* "I latched on to a young folksinger a few months ago who I just think is going to be absolutely a giant. He's Bruce Springsteen, a good Catholic boy from New Jersey. He's one of the greatest talents I've ever come across." The agreement was between CBS and Laurel Canyon Productions owned by Mike Appel and Jim Cretecos, to whom Springsteen had imprudently granted complete control over everything: songs, recordings, and rights of all kinds. It was a terrible deal, at least for Springsteen. His managers, on the other hand, got three dollars (in royalties) every time he got one.

34-35 *John Hammond, the legendary record producer who worked with Billie Holiday and Bob Dylan, in his office.*

TO SPRINGSTEEN,
NEW JERSEY IS
ASBURY PARK.
AND THAT'S WHERE
IT ALL BEGAN.

1973

36 *The cover of* Greetings from Asbury Park, N.J.

37 *Springsteen, wearing a shirt with the Triumph logo, 1974.*

But money was the furthest thing from his mind. Springsteen had reached the tipping point, the plot twist: the recording of his first real album. Between June and October, Springsteen created *Greetings from Asbury Park, N.J.*, his first album with a band assembled by him just for the occasion, made up of the musicians that he was most familiar with, including Clarence Clemons on saxophone. It was no E Street Band, but things were starting to come together.

The recordings were done on the cheap, at 914 Sound Studios, during the last week of June. Once the sessions had wrapped up, the disagreements began: Appel and Hammond had met Springsteen as a solo artist, and they preferred his singer-songwriter side and the recordings of him alone. Springsteen knew himself, his past and his dreams, and he loved the songs recorded with the band. They reached a compromise: five songs with the band, and five without. When Clive Davis listened to them, however, he wasn't entirely sure: he thought the album lacked a powerful single. Springsteen didn't lose heart and, in just a few weeks, he wrote two new songs, *Blinded by the Light* and *Spirit in the Night*. They were recorded on September 11, 1972, as a trio: Vini Lopez on drums, Springsteen on bass, guitar, and piano, and, last but not least, Clarence Clemons on sax. Davis embraced the new tracks enthusiastically, giving them free rein. The album was a particularly flavorful appetizer of what was to come. On it are tracks that would go down in history,

two written and recorded at the last minute—the two that best express what was happening, how Springsteen was changing, how he found a new formula that mixes rock, soul, and singer-songwriter genres, with refined yet passionate sonorous impact. Tracks like "For You," "Growin' Up," "Lost in the Flood," the legendary "It's Hard to Be a Saint in the City," all with the band, plus the more intimate "Mary Queen of Arkansas" and "The Angel." And it's all wrapped up with a cover that leaves no doubt as to the sense of belonging that Springsteen wants to convey, not just with the title of the album, but also with its artwork. It's New Jersey, it's Asbury Park, it's his house, his world, his life.

There are a lot of songs, many of which are still part of the playlist of any Springsteen marathon, and over the years the album will be looked at in a new light. But not everything is perfect, not everything is balanced. First of all, it's still an album that focuses too much on his folk-singer side rather than his rock soul, and the production by Appel and Cretecos doesn't do justice to the impact of the live band; everything seems too toned down. But it's still a great album. At least they thought so over at Columbia, which, between October 1972 and January 1973, prepared to release the album and distribute it in record stores. The album was a flop. Just a few thousand copies sold. It got good reviews, but they don't make much of a difference. Lester Bangs himself dubbed it a mix between the lyrics of Bob Dylan and the band and voice of Van Morrison.

The best thing to come out of the album, at least for Springsteen at the time, was the basic formation of the E Street Band, and a Harley Davidson he bought with the money from Columbia. He spent the rest on alcohol. It wasn't exactly a stellar outcome. Quite the opposite. The first tour was even worse. Columbia put them as the opening act for Chicago, an experience so ill-fated that he vowed never to open for anyone else ever again.

38-39 *Springsteen and the complete band (from left: Clarence Clemons, Bruce Springsteen, David Sancious, Vini Lopez, Danny Federici, and Garry Tallent), on the Jersey Shore in August 1973.*

BRUCE SPRINGSTEEN: THE WILD, THE INNOCENT & THE E STREET SHUFFLE

conveyed through particularly original lyrics and sounds. Stories that, as Clemons put it: "There were endless stories, because Bruce was working on them constantly, never stopping, and, by the way, they were beautiful too. Here and there he'd sneak in more introspective elements or nuances that made those characters truly believable."

They aren't only "endless"; there are also lots of them, because as of June 1973 (when the tour with Chicago ended), they started playing in the studio again, and Bruce began writing track after track. The album is consistent in its themes and sound, created as an album, not just one-off tracks, with its own natural sequence. Springsteen, Clemons, Tallent, Federici, Vini Lopez, and the fundamental David Sancious gave substance to the sound of the band, the E Street Band, a name suggested by Sancious, but also a relationship built upon friendship, similarities, and brotherhood, which made everything particularly heartfelt. Absolute masterpieces make the album a gem, especially "Rosalita (Come Out Tonight)," a sort of autobiography that quickly became the heart of their concerts, with its seven minutes of music that easily became more when played live. It was a theatrical show in rock form, a fast-moving

And while 1972 was the perfect year, 1973 seemed to have nothing to give to Springsteen. Once the tour with Chicago ended, Columbia wanted to try again and, in record time, in November 1973, just a few months after the first, a second album was released: *The Wild, the Innocent & the E Street Shuffle*. It was the album that Springsteen needed to make things clear: he'd had enough of folk songs and acoustic guitars. Rock took center stage with soul at its core, a romantic album that nonetheless contains wonderful ballads. But it was the storytelling that shone brightest,

40 and 41 *Above: the cover of* The Wild, the Innocent & the E Street Shuffle; *opposite: a portrait from the same photo shoot.*

film, a complete musical from start to finish, with a sense of humor that made it all entirely explosive. And then the ultra-romantic "4th of July, Asbury Park (Sandy)," presented by the record label as a love ballad "that redefines street romanticism and definitively contributes to the birth of an idealized vision of the Jersey Shore." Springsteen wrote it in an apartment carved out of a garage that he lived in with his girlfriend, imagining it as "a good-bye to my adopted hometown and the life I'd lived there before I recorded. Sandy was a composite of some of the girls I'd known along the Shore. I used the boardwalk and the closing down of the town as a metaphor for the end of a summer romance and the changes I was experiencing in my own life."

And then there were the narrative formulas of "Kitty's Back" and "Wild Billy's Circus Story," still in a singer-songwriter vein, and two more masterpieces, "New York City Serenade," a tribute to the Big Apple, and "Incident on 57th Street," with so many fascinating, well-defined characters, Billy and his lover Diamond Jackie, the vibraphonist that plays the trash can, or the refined junk dealer, up to the "Fish Lady," in the heart of the song, that the protagonist tries to redeem. "I took on a theme that I would return to," Springsteen explained. "The search for redemption. Over the next twenty years I'd work this one as only a good Catholic boy could have." The critics were happy, but the sales were disappointing. Again. For a label like Columbia, two albums that weren't hits was a clear enough sign, one that managed to transform the enthusiasm for the "new Bob Dylan" who had been signed in record time into lukewarm tolerance. So lukewarm that "The Wild," "The Innocent" and "The E Street Shuffle" weren't put out as singles. Not much more could be done. The answer was the same as always, when facing obstacles and problems: play more concerts.

42-43 *A cheery Springsteen, posing on the Jersey Shore in August 1973.*

44-45 One of the most classic portraits of
Springsteen, taken by Michael Ochs in 1978.

2

1974–1984
BORN
TO RUN

WITH HIS GUITAR AND HIS BAND, **SPRINGSTEEN FOREVER BECAME** A "PRISONER OF ROCK 'N' ROLL"

It would take two long years of hard work for Mike Appel to turn things around. Two years of concerts, venues snatched up on the cheap, promises of success and what were effectively marathon shows, the kind that would become Springsteen's signature, layman's ceremonies with a faint air of Catholic holiness, tempered by stories about women, sex, and rebellion. There was even a new drummer, Ernest "Boom" Carter,

On May 9, 1974, in Boston, Jon Landau saw "the future of rock 'n' roll."

who brought a whole new rhythm to those events, events that went well beyond the very concept of what a rock concert was at the time. They were so engaging that, despite Springsteen being in the good graces of music critics already, when he played as the opening act for Bonnie Raitt at the Harvard Square Theater on May 9, 1974, Jon Landau wrote in *The Real Paper* the most famous words of his career and one of the most well-known reviews in the history of music criticism: "I saw rock and roll's future and its name is Bruce Springsteen. On a night when I needed to feel young, he made me feel like I was hearing music for the very first time. When his two-hour set ended, I could only think, can anyone really be this good; can anyone say this much to me, can rock 'n' roll speak with this kind of power and glory?"

That paved the way for true change. For about six years, Springsteen had been working seriously as a musician, two albums had been released without much success, but one thing was clear: everything worked live. So, for people to buy records, first they had to go to a live show, and the band had to perform to its fullest. Instead of seeking ever-better musicians, Springsteen began searching for ever-better light and audio engineers. The concerts made a qualitative leap: they became colossal shows that didn't just present Springsteen's oeuvre, but also covers and rock classics. After a promising 1972 and a disappointing 1973, 1974 was the year of live shows, one that ended with giving it their all, playing five nights at the Bottom Line in New York, with two performances per night. Ten concerts (by Bruce Springsteen) in five days. There were still ten more years until the global explosion of Boss mania, but this was where the foundations were laid. And it was also the backdrop to the 1975 release of *Born to Run*.

Up until that point, Springsteen's career had been a matter of stamina and endurance, a sort of music marathon that involved playing—a lot—with explosive energy for a growing audience. It was the weapon to advance with. Quality, sure, but what impressed people most was the quantity. A true tireless rock workhorse that, when *Born to Run* was released, transformed into a complete artist, a deep, unique singer-songwriter. Not just an uproarious rock god, but a voice of America, its history, culture, dreams, and tears, its streets and alleyways, splendor and perdition. The America of the

American dream, but also the other side of the coin, the eternal hope for redemption, rebirth, and possibility; deep, working-class America, vital and real; the America of those who have lost, not just those who have won; the America of those who are "born to run," even if they've lived in the same town their entire life and have only a vague notion of what the rest of the world is like.

This time, Jon Landau was by his side, crossing over from music critic to friend, then becoming his producer and manager. Moreover, at Springsteen's side was a band that evolved as they recorded. Ernest Carter, Vinnie Lopez, and David Sancious left; Roy Bittan and Max Weinberg arrived. And, coming in through what we might call a back door (seeing as he joined the band only after the album was recorded, appearing substantially only in the role of a "friend"), Steve Van Zandt joined Tallent, Clemons, and Federici to become the legendary E Street Band.

At that time, Van Zandt was a band member and manager of Southside Johnny & the Asbury Jukes, who had just the sound that Springsteen was after. So, he asked (again, in the studio as a "friend") Van Zandt to manage the wind instruments, to explain what they were supposed to do and how. Now, they weren't musicians trained at the conservatory, so those explanations came in the form of a vocal imitation of what the various band members were supposed to play. It worked. Plus, Van Zandt, as Springsteen himself has said, "saved" the riff of *Born to Run*, suggesting a minor chord that literally changed the cards on the table.

48 *Springsteen playing at the Trenton War Memorial in New Jersey, November 1974.*

51 *Steve Van Zandt, the guitarist and singer, photographed in Holmdel, New Jersey on October 17, 1979.*

SAXOPHONE," THE EMPEROR OF THE E STREET BAND.

And then there was Clarence Clemons: "Previous to *Born to Run*, Clarence was just the very large, gifted black saxophonist in my band," says Springsteen in his autobiography. "After *Born to Run*, our stage show changed also . . . the crowd lit up when we simply walked toward each other and planted ourselves center stage." Clemons had become the "Big Man on the saxophone," he was the "Emperor of E Street," the "brother" that Springsteen leans on in the legendary album cover. "We were incongruent, missing pieces to an old and unresolved puzzle, two longing halves of an eccentric and potent whole," Springsteen continues in his book. The relationship between the two of them would be fundamental to the growth of the band, but also to him personally.

52-53 *Clemons and Springsteen playing on stage during an E Street Band concert.*

Everything was perfect, but that didn't mean that Springsteen was satisfied. The band's recording sessions were brutal ,and the early versions of the album ended up thrown out on the street (the first) and chucked out of the window of his hotel room and into a river (the second). It would take the surprise release of a few tracks by Mike Appel and the great reception that they got to persuade Springsteen to free the album in August of that year. To record it, he had a notable budget—and the last chance he'd get. He headed into the studio in early May 1974 and he left near the end of June 1975, almost fourteen months, many of which he was working on just one song, "Born to Run," the title track. But it isn't just any song. It's *the* song. If there's a track that defines Springsteen post-1975, it's "Born to Run," with its epic romantic tale, encapsulating failure, redemption, and success, with the narrator's humble start and great success, no matter the odds, in spite of fate, destiny, society, and the world. Because he, the singer-subject, which

Failure, redemption, and success, Springsteen and Wendy in "Born to Run" were exactly that.

it's hard not to identify as Springsteen himself and which millions of people, every day, identify with, and Wendy, two vagabond souls, were "born to run." It's the essence of the romantic dream of rock 'n' roll, with Springsteen's guitar dominating and the sound of the band that supports him; it's the song sung in chorus when everything is about to be lost; it's the song sung by crowds at concerts, giving life to a community in which we're all brothers, everyone has hope, everyone knows that no matter how terrible life is, it is meant to be lived to the fullest.

We could say that *Born to Run* is a concept album, each side opens with odes to escapes and redemption, e.g. "Thunder Road" and "Born to Run," and each one ends with songs that have a sad backdrop, talking about defeat, loss, betrayal, e.g. "Jungleland" and "Backstreets." And it's in this incredible contrast between hope and failure, between the unstoppable vitality of some tracks and the bitterness of others, that we find the "truth" of the album and its ability to speak to such a wide audience. It embodies Springsteen's "truth."

The album is a dense concentrate of old and modern rock. Considering that rock had reached a critical turning point with the crisis of prog and the birth of punk, Springsteen appeared on the scene to offer salvation and redemption even to rock music itself. He's the one to pull it out from the abyss of spectacle, easy listening, and its most out-there progressive tendencies, and bring it back to the streets, to blood, sweat, and tears, to the joy of having fun, to sex and carnal desire. Is there anything new in all that? No. But, as Greil Marcus wrote in his review of the album for *Rolling Stone,* "It is the drama that counts; the stories Springsteen is telling are nothing new, though no one has ever told them better or made them matter more."

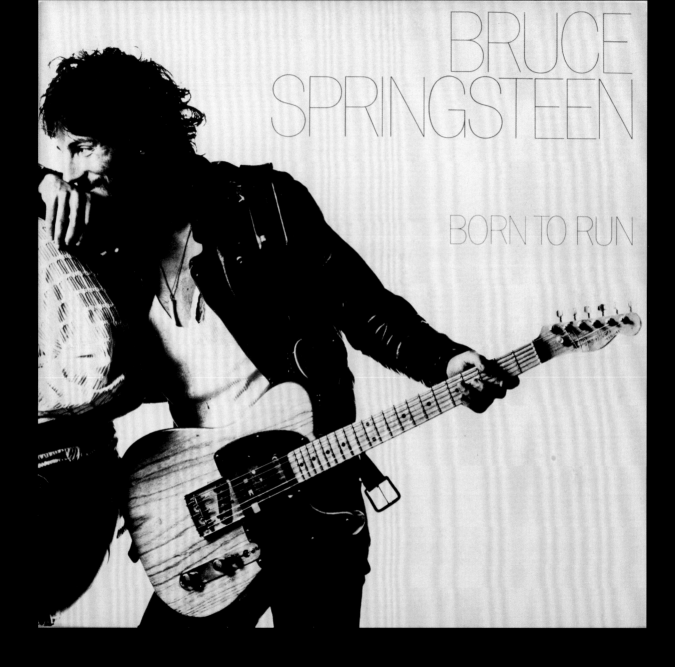

What *Born to Run* contains was quite different than what an audience that had never been to a Springsteen concert could have imagined. The voice was grittier, there was more emphasis and a much more targeted, calibrated sound. It was a real album. Even Columbia Records "got" it, and invested in its release this time. The label put $250,000 on the line, plastering Springsteen's face everywhere, including on the now-famous covers of *Newsweek* and *Time* (in the same month!). The Springsteen iconography was born, and all the now-famous elements of his brand had crystallized, including his most iconic guitar. It was immortalized for the first time ever on the album cover, even if it had been with him for a few years by then.

It's an electric guitar from the 1950s, a composite Fender with a Telecaster body and an Esquire neck that he bought in 1971 from Phil Petillo's store for $185. It's the guitar of "I got this guitar, and I learned how to make it talk" that Springsteen has never let go of, an idol that has constantly cropped up on his album covers, recordings, and, of course, live sets.

56 *In October 1975, two of America's biggest weekly magazines featured Springsteen on the cover, "rock's new sensation."*

57 *Springsteen's "hybrid" 1971 Fender, with a Telecaster body and an Esquire neck.*

The story of the guitar itself, even before belonging to Springsteen and thus definitively being delivered to its destiny, is incredible. Its provenance was first plotted out by David Eichelbaum, a Fender expert who studied the matter at length, and later by Petillo, who sold it and also repaired it over the years. Eichelbaum claimed that the neck came from an Esquire with just one pick-up, a version of the classic two-pickup Telecaster, judging from the sticker that probably dates to 1957. Petillo, on the other hand, said the body came from a guitar owned by a record label and was modified as part of a scam. It has four pickups and two output jacks to record on separate channels, so that it would seem like the performer was recording four different versions of the same solo, and thus would be paid much more.

To make room for all those electronics, various parts under the pickguard were hollowed out, so that when Petillo removed the extra parts they remained empty. On its own, the Telecaster was lightweight, but once it had been routed out, it was ultra-light, just the guitar to use for marathon concerts, weighing only as much as an acoustic guitar. Not only that, but it could be played under water because Petillo had modified it in his shop, making it practically waterproof with silicone gaskets and stainless-steel and titanium hardware.

That very guitar was used and abused constantly from 1973 until 2005. It broke over and over again, and over and over again it was repaired by Petillo. At times, in the middle of a tour, it was shipped off in an airplane on its own, to be fixed and sent back in time for the next date of the tour. It only got to retire because a lifetime with Springsteen had worn it down to the point that it risked damage beyond repair. Today it's used exclusively for truly special recordings and concerts.

Many claim that, thanks to its unique construction, its history, the way in which Springsteen made use of it, and even its presence in a few of the most famous images in the history of music, it's the most valuable guitar in the world, estimated to be worth between one and five million dollars. That is, if it were for sale: Springsteen has said more than once that it will be buried with him.

In 1975, the "Springsteen model" was a mix of cutthroat touring and three-to-four-hour concerts; wild, fanatical feedback from music critics; and massive investment by record labels. In spite of all this, the album's reception was noteworthy, but not resounding. A million copies sold and it took third place on the charts. But the tour's tickets sold out quicker than ever, marking a net divide between album sales and the success of Springsteen's live shows, a divide that would be with him and the band for a few more years to come.

LIVE, SPRINGSTEEN IS EXPLOSIVE, joining the Olympus of rock through THE MAIN ENTRANCE

Up until this point, the hardest part of being a musician, for Springsteen, was interacting with other musicians, avoiding band breakups due to excessive infighting, and finding people he could effectively work with. From *Born to Run* onward, the main problem became living the life of a star, forming a major contrast in the propulsive part of his career: he had grown up with certain ideas, standing tall with a specific image of what music is and how it should be artfully executed. Suddenly he became an investment for a record label that, at least in part, managed his public image in order to maximize profits. And if he never got along with the nuns when he was an easily impressionable boy, he certainly wasn't going to get along with record label execs at twenty-six.

58 *A picture of Springsteen on the stage of the Hammersmith Odeon in London, the E Street Band's first concert outside of the US.*

BY NOVEMBER 1975, LONDON WAS READY FOR BRUCE SPRINGSTEEN.

The first resounding incident took place in London, revolving around the November concerts he played at the Hammersmith Odeon. Unbeknownst to Springsteen, Columbia Records had covered the city with posters that read: "Finally London is Ready for Bruce Springsteen!" They were squeezing him for all he was worth, treating him like one of the myriad other musicians to walk all over, day and night, with marketing that's out of his control. Springsteen ripped all the posters he could from the walls and played a good part of the concert with his back to the audience. He had been known for having that type of personality, and it was high time that the record labels got a taste of it too. Likewise, it was high time for him to learn the value of a dollar.

60-61 *Springsteen looking at the marquee announcing his arrival, above the entrance to the Hammersmith Odeon In London, before his first concert in England on November 18, 1975.*

Despite being a successful musician, famous enough to be on big magazine covers, he was still earning $350 a week, as stipulated in the original deal he had signed years before. He only had a few thousand dollars in the bank. So, for the first time, he read the contract he had signed with Columbia. The result was a ten-month lawsuit with Appel and a year of being effectively banned from the recording studio. No matter, the answer was to play even more live shows for all of 1976, after which he had so many new ideas that his own albums weren't enough. In the late 1970s, Springsteen began writing for his peers: Manfred Mann's Earth Band covered "Blinded by the Light" in 1977; one year later, Patti Smith received "Because the Night" as a gift (so to speak); the year after that, the Pointer Sisters played "Fire" (which Springsteen still hadn't recorded at the time), not to mention the four tracks composed for Van Zandt's Southside Johnny & The Asbury Jukes.

One other knock-on effect of the lawsuit was a change in management and, after a few years in which it was unofficial, in 1975 Landau signed his contract with Springsteen, officially becoming his manager in 1977. To celebrate, they began the recording session for *Darkness on the Edge of Town*, a more stripped-down, gloomier album, permeated by foreboding but full of classic tracks. Everything around Springsteen was changing—he himself, but also the masses of people who were his fans (due to his success), and even music in general. Punk had exploded, rock had "died" once again, and new wave was on its way in.

1 9 7 8

Springsteen knew it, and he also knew that he couldn't ignore the end of a world, that of the 1970s, with the failure of the youth culture that had dreamed of changing things yet ultimately never managed to do so. Punks sang cynically about having no future, others painted the world and music black, reducing it to the bare essentials and stripping it of any and all embellishment. Springsteen responded in his own way, seeking out the *Darkness on the Edge of Town*, the perfect title to bring his world into the new world. The album is a masterpiece, a deep, monumental album, starting from the first track, "Badlands," which pushes the disc upward, in a glorious ode to freedom, rebellion, and faith. "I believe in the love that you gave me / I believe in the faith that can save me / I believe in the hope and I pray / That someday it may raise me / Above these / Badlands." It's sung with the audience to make it become true, like a prayer. Fans sang it then, in 1978, and they still sing it with Springsteen at his concerts today, because it never comes true, because life betrays, yet hope remains. What followed was a string of hits, with the E Street Band complete and in full force for the first time, with Jon Landau producing and Jimmy Iovine as the engineer, abandoning the wall of sound of *Born to Run*, to land in an unprecedented, resounding place that was dense, pulsating, and essential. That took him from the pop of "Prove It All Night" to the moving romanticism of "Something in the Night," from the future heralded by "Promised Land" to that lost in "Racing in the Street," touching upon the Biblical story of "Adam Raised a Cain" to the bitter, gloomy tale of "Darkness on the Edge of Town." He wrote a massive number of songs at the time, recording many and tossing many out. To the point that he even decided not to include "Because the Night" on the album, discarding it. It may sound crazy, but it's true. It was eventually "saved" by Patti Smith, who turned it into her most famous, beloved single, changing some of the lyrics.

62 *The cover of* Darkness on the Edge of Town, *Springsteen's 1978 album.*

"WELL I BELIEVE IN THE LOVE THAT YOU GAVE ME, I BELIEVE IN THE FAITH THAT COULD SAVE ME, I BELIEVE IN HOPE."

64 *Bruce Springsteen playing with the E Street Band at the Fox Theater in Atlanta, Georgia, on November 1, 1978.*

It was hard to resist the cyclone that Springsteen and his band brought to the stage with this new repertoire, mixed with that of the past. This time, the tour included eighty-three dates and 118 concerts lasting almost four hours each. A demonstration of athleticism and endurance rarely seen at the time, which ended on New Year's Eve in 1979. Springsteen closed out the 1970s—his and that of rock—with a show in Cleveland that culminated in him dancing on a 26-foot (8 m) high stack of speakers, while yelling our opening motto: "I'm just a prisoner of rock 'n' roll" (see page 9). It's the first act of a period defined by exponential growth. And once it was over, it was immortalized in a live collection that documents a decade, from 1975 to 1985, not just of Springsteen, but of rock history (in addition to instantly burying the dozens of bootlegs that had come out in the meantime). In some way, those ten years marked a golden standard in terms of live performances, becoming a yardstick for everyone from that point on.

The Seventies ended with two triumphant performances, a golden decade for his concerts.

67 *Springsteen sitting on an amplifier on the stage of the Ahoy in Rotterdam, April 29, 1981.*

Bruce Springsteen doesn't do drugs. At least that's what he's always claimed, and no one has ever said otherwise. No drugs, of any kind, light or hard. He's a more "I'm high on life" or "The real party is on stage" type of guy. And unlike countless others, he's shown what it truly means to constantly be hopped up on life; and also, unlike many others, he's been truly tough on anyone in his band or on his staff whose behavior or attitude might distract him from the tour or his musical commitments. Meaning that, if the musicians around him wanted to do drugs, they had to do it in secret. Once, before a concert in Boston that was part of the *Darkness on the Edge of Town* tour, Springsteen burst into Clemons's bus, the bus known for being the party bus (Springsteen's, on the other hand, was known as the "quiet bus"), walking in on various members of the band sniffing cocaine. He walked out with a dry "If I see this shit again one more time, I don't care who's responsible, they're out of the band." And he meant it. He really was prepared to say goodbye to even the most important, long-time band members for behavior of the sort.

He doesn't and didn't do drugs, but for a very, very long time he was addicted to women. Lots of them. And he didn't just have them; he talked about them. In fact, he made it a habit to talk about his sexual exploits, lust after them, and then talk about them again, before moving on to others.

69 *A portrait of Springsteen taking a break from the sound check of the concert at Alex Cooley's Electric Ballroom in Atlanta, Georgia on August 22, 1975.*

In 1979, he was sued for $3 million by an ex-girlfriend who he humiliated on stage. But the lawsuit was settled quickly and the sum paid in haste. The event happened on the stage of the No Nukes concerts series, the first big anti-nuclear concerts in the world, organized by Jackson Browne just after the accident at the Three Mile Island nuclear plant, the worst in America.

Incidentally, the No Nukes concerts also contained the first inklings of ethical and civil awareness for Springsteen. His songs had always contained a form of individualism that only allowed social commentary to be read between the lines, but No Nukes became the first of many public events that promoted his personal ideals. It was a very long road that would lead him to political activism, starting in 2000. Moreover, like everything that matters in Springsteen's life, even that commitment was measured on stage, the only language he truly speaks, the only one that he has mastered, the only one that he feels able to express himself with. Despite his songs always appearing first on a studio album, it was during his live shows that what Springsteen had to say really became concrete. And even the songs with the most meaningful lyrics never have a "political" life until they've been played and heard during a concert.

The No Nukes concert series gave rise to a documentary film, which was also the first official audio-visual recording of Springsteen's famed stage performance. Like the worldwide broadcast of the wedding of Queen Elizabeth II and Prince Philip, for the first time people across the planet gained access to the performance of the most important member of the royal rock 'n' roll family, in the very act that consecrated his nobility.

The entire decade that was starting for Springsteen would be defined by two parallel worlds: a very dark, increasingly lonely career, juxtaposed with live shows of a size, vastness, frequency, and media reach that was constantly expanding; benefit concerts and a private life that tried, and failed, to find balance. As always, it was expressed, narrated, and sometimes even born on stage or during a live performance. His life was increasingly there, traveling the world, and less and less at home. In fact, he didn't even own one, despite being a millionaire.

THE 1980S BEGAN WITH A DOUBLE ALBUM, *THE RIVER*, A PASSIONATE POLITICAL MASTERPIECE, FULLY CHARGED WITH ROCK MUSIC AND EMOTION.

So, 1980 began with *The River*, twenty tracks soaked in a precise political outlook, and a tour that took him to Australia (where he was worshipped like a god) and Japan (where he had to cut his concerts short due to a 9 pm event curfew) for the first time. Those were the years in which music concerts began to become marketing machines, where money was made through ticket sales, sure, but mainly via merchandising and the sale of T-shirts right outside of the arena. Springsteen made sure that didn't happen at his.

The River is an openly political album that tells the classic tales of the working class. However, they're no longer the product of individual choices, but rather destinies determined by the social system around them (the perfect example of this is exemplified by the protagonists of the title track, a story inspired by his sister Virginia and her husband, whose lives were dominated by the lack of alternatives).

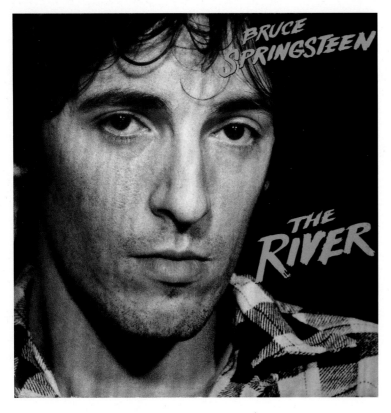

Its unexpected success was in part thanks to "Hungry Heart," a single that was the first truly massive track of his career. If we were to stop there, as many often do, the album would be seen in a distorted light. *The River* was only slightly brighter than *Darkness on the Edge of Town*, and it certainly is in its sound, in the lineup of an E Street Band that he managed with expert artistry and which proved to be pliable in a laudable way.

However, the same can't be said of its stories, of the tales of lives from the lower rungs of the social ladder in the United States, the one that seems incapable of imagining that change is possible. A collection of interrupted existences which for the most part echo the "no future" that England's rockers had sung about just a few years prior, but without the nihilism of punk, even more loaded with feelings, passion, maybe even pain, but also life. It's a long, hour-and-a-half double album with twenty tracks, so there's room for a bit of simple fun too, with the rousing rock 'n' roll of "Cadillac Ranch," the rhythm of "Ramrod," and a track that flirts with vintage pop, the aforementioned "Hungry Hearts." There's room for the dreams of "Independence Day" or for the immense nocturnal love of "Drive All Night" ("I swear I'll drive all night again, just to buy you some shoes"), or the passionate love of "Two Hearts."

But at its heart the album is bitter: it's that of a dramatic ballad like *The River* (with the harmonica at the beginning that seems to quote Ennio Morricone, one of Springsteen's favorites), a formerly rich river where dreams and hopes once flowed, but which now has run dry. It's that of the resignation of "Point Blank," the boredom of "Stolen Car"; and even the street— the highway that to Springsteen was a symbol of opportunity and escape to a better future—becomes a backdrop to death in "Wreck on the Highway."

At the end of 1980, *Rolling Stone* named him the artist of the year, the first of three consecutive times that would happen. The early 1980s marked a dizzying rise to fame that would lead to *Born in the U.S.A.* and,

in some way, close a chapter of his life. In 1981, his nine-week tour would visit ten countries and, for the first time, his British dates were a resounding success.

The River was the first attempt, a mostly successful one at that, to square the circle between the power, force, and emotion of his live shows and the sound of his albums. Springsteen wanted to bridge the gap, but he also wanted to reinvent himself and his music. Yes, he was still a "prisoner of rock 'n' roll," but at the end of the day he was also a singer-songwriter. What was missing was the right balance between the two, between the undeniable entertainment of his shows and the strength of the tales he told, which were increasingly personal, intimate, emotional, social, and political.

That's what his right hand was doing, his more commercial hand. The left hand, on the other side, the more socially minded one, pushed him to play six concerts in a row in Los Angeles, the proceeds of which went to charity, more precisely, the Vietnam Veterans of America. In 1980, something happened that influenced the way he saw war. Up until then, Springsteen had been a boy terrified of dying in Vietnam, one who had narrowly avoided the draft in Freehold. But in 1980, at just under thirty years old and touring the US, while on the outskirts of Phoenix in a run-down drugstore, he bought *Born on the Fourth of July*, the book by Ron Kovic which recounted the author's experience as an infantryman in Southeast Asia. Just two weeks later, Springsteen found himself in Los Angeles, in a hotel for micro-celebrities; and there, near the pool, sitting in a wheelchair, was Kovic himself. It had taken two weeks for Springsteen to devour the book and change his mind on a lot of things; yet it was Kovic who walked over, introduced himself, and offered to take Springsteen to meet a few veterans in Venice Beach. They were all drug addicts, homeless, and stricken by post-traumatic stress syndrome. The event was one that left a mark and, along with the biography of Woody Guthrie (the one written by Joe Klein), it led him to *Nebraska* and, later on, *Born in the U.S.A.*

In 1980, Springsteen bought *Born on the Fourth of July* by Ron Kovic, and his view of the Vietnam War and the US changed forever.

75 *The cover of* Nebraska, *the album released on September 30, 1982.*

Nebraska was even more challenging and further from his other albums, including *The River:* "*Nebraska* began as an unintended meditation on my childhood and its mysteries. I had no conscious political agenda or social theme. I was after a feeling, a tone that felt like the world I'd known and still carried inside me. The remnants of that world were only ten minutes and ten miles from where I was living. The ghosts of *Nebraska* were drawn from my many sojourns into the small-town streets I'd grown up on. [...] I wanted black bedtime stories. I thought of the records of John Lee Hooker and Robert Johnson, music that sounded so good with the lights out. These songs were the opposite of the rock music I'd been writing. They were restrained, still on the surface, with a world of moral ambiguity and unease below."

Springsteen recorded all the songs alone. Just him and his guitar. Then he went back to the studio with the band and fine-tuned them, but he soon realized that the "arranged" versions were worse, that they lost their authenticity and strength. So as not to destroy the essence of that which he had done, he decided to directly release the demos. It was a return to folk music in some ways, and as such the two books he had just read (*Born on the Fourth of July* and the biography of Woody Guthrie) also found a place on the same album. At that point in his career, a less-mainstream album wouldn't have been the end of the world. To the contrary, it could even help shape Springsteen's image before going back to his more popular sound on the following album. Yet *Nebraska* was a surprise success, easily rising to the top ten charts. It was a sign that something had changed in how Springsteen was seen, such a leap that even his new, more "challenging" album flew off the shelves. Boss mania was just around the corner.

> The "ghosts" of Nebraska came from the roads where Springsteen grew up, music to listen to with the lights off, the exact opposite of the rock 'n' roll he'd written up until then.

While two books influenced *Nebraska*, film (and storytelling) was what influenced Springsteen's 1983. *Wise Blood* by John Huston struck him and pushed him to read the novel by Flannery O'Connor that the film is based on. It's a travel tale set in the American South, the story of a preacher who ends up among the worst sinners there are. Around that same time, Springsteen also saw *Badlands*, the first film by Terrence Malick, a triumph of youthful rebellion with Martin Sheen and Sissy Spacek. It seemed to have come straight out of one of his songs, the tale of kids who are different than the world they live in, who just want to leave. They're two stories in which religion comes into play in different ways. It's more obvious in the first, seeing that a preacher is one of the protagonists, while in the latter, everything is transfigured through the eyes of Malick (who's Catholic, no less). But, while *Wise Blood* impressed him, *Badlands* was a eureka moment. He had to talk to Malick directly. He had his people get in contact with the director, because he needed to discuss those fragments of real life of the characters, the ones before they run away, moments of failure and desperation, crime and irrelevance. Springsteen's darkest moment is at the doorstep. It could already be felt on *The River* and *Nebraska*, but now it's reached a whole new level. Before the end of 1983, he headed out with his friend Matty Delia in a blue Chevrolet Camaro for a trip that, for once, isn't a tour, but a private pilgrimage.

Curiously, it's once again a journey from the East Coast to the West Coast. From the old house in New Jersey to the new mini-mansion he rented in the Hollywood Hills. The two hit all the most marginalized states on back roads, stopping at the motels with the worst neon signs, and, as Springsteen tells it, boosting José Cuervo tequila's stock listing price by at least ten percentage points. It all seemed wonderful, but it was the product of ghosts and demons, the fruit of the desire to get away to clear his head, the result (according to Springsteen) of depression. He began seeing a psychiatrist, a habit he'd never give up and which, more than once, saved him from the abyss.

78 and 79 Two images from Springsteen's first European tour in 1975.
Opposite: Springsteen on stage in London. Above: in Rotterdam with Clarence
Clemons and Steve Van Zandt.

ON STAGE,
SPRINGSTEEN
IS A SINGER,
A SONGWRITER,
A PREACHER,
A ROCKER,
A PROPHET.

82 and 83 *Four snapshots of Springsteen live,*
taken by Michael Putland.

84 Springsteen on stage at the Winterland Ballroom in San Francisco, California, in
December 1978.

85 Clarence Clemons and Bruce Springsteen with the E Street Band while touring
the West Coast of the US in 1978.

86 *The Darkness Tour was the name given to the series of concerts played in 1978 to promote the release of* Darkness on the Edge of Town.

87 *Springsteen in concert in 1979 at the Los Angeles Sports Arena.*

88 and 89 *Springsteen conquers Europe with his 1981 tour. The photographs on these two pages were taken in Rotterdam that year.*

3

1984–1991
BORN IN THE U.S.A.
AND GLOBAL SUCCESS

A LEGEND BEGINS.
SEVEN YEARS WITH JUST ONE MISSION
SAVE ROCK 'N' ROLL

It's hard to separate *Nebraska* from the follow-up album, *Born in the U.S.A.:* if you look at the time and the way in which they were made, they're two incredibly different—but closely connected—albums. As we said, *Nebraska* was recorded with the E Street Band, then Springsteen changed his mind and used the demos he recorded alone. *Born in the U.S.A.* started out as a solo recording, but with the idea of playing it as a band, once again in 1982. The first half of *Born in the U.S.A.* was recorded at the same time as *Nebraska,* and they were meant to be released together. But it was clear that they were two different storylines, two different lives, two different worlds.

In Los Angeles, Springsteen had a recording studio built and, for five months, he worked on the second part of the album by himself, trying to complete it, inspired by a script that had been sent to him by director Paul Schrader. In 1987, that script would become the film *Light of Day,* with a song of the same name by Springsteen. For the demos of *Born in the U.S.A.,* he played all the instruments on all the tracks and, where he couldn't manage, he got a bit of help from a drum machine. However, his depression and that deep dive into the America of those years,

In *Born in the U.S.A.*, there's no hope, only the bitterness of shattered dreams.

years in which "many left and few came back," boiled over here too. Especially in the title track, which is perhaps one of the most misunderstood songs ever, perhaps the most obvious example of instrumentals speaking a much clearer language than words can ever hope to. The lyrics of "Born in the U.S.A." are unambiguous, a harsh indictment of how the country treats veterans and, more generally, the common working-class man. It's a track with dramatic bitterness; it's the song in which all the hope that Springsteen so often sings about, all the speeding cars, all the escapes, all the dreams, are erased in just one phrase: "Nowhere to run ain't got nowhere to go."

BORN IN THE U.S.A./BRUCE SPRINGSTEEN

But the instrumentals are so powerful, so positive, with the sound of a stadium anthem, that they overpower the intended meaning and turn the song, for many, into a symbol of America singing its own praises. And this time the album didn't sell two million copies or even five million, but eighteen million. A new triumph for Springsteen. At the top of all the charts. Seven singles spread out for at least a year of releases. And of course, the iconic album art (a backside, jeans and a flag in the background) doesn't exactly clue us in to the true meaning of the lead track. Instead, it's more of a reflection of the hedonism of the Reagan years. Reagan himself even joined the masses in misunderstanding its message and referred to the track (used at his rallies) as an

SPRINGSTEEN DIDN'T IDENTIFY WITH
RONALD REAGAN'S AMERICA
and the album says it loud and clear

example of hope in America. The very same Reagan who Springsteen had attacked from his pulpit of a stage during a concert a few years earlier, held on the night the President was elected. The same Reagan that Springsteen declared he was firmly against two nights after the rally in which he had been dragged into the picture, from a concert stage in Pittsburgh (and on what other occasion, if not that one!?), wondering, and asking the audience, what album he loves the most. Perhaps *Nebraska?* With that, he launched into "Johnny 99," a hard-hitting song about factory closures and a worker who, having lost his job, ends up in prison for having shot a watchman. But it was all in vain.

95 *The inner sleeve of* Born in the U.S.A., *with the full E Street Band.*

Bruce Springsteen

Steve Van Zandt

Roy Bittan

Garry Tallent

Max Weinberg

Danny Federici

Clarence Clemons

The E Street Band

The point is that Springsteen had changed, and so had his image. He constantly sought out the adrenaline of stadiums and concerts, even when he wasn't on stage, but he didn't give in to drugs. Instead, he started working out, becoming quite devoted about it. He got big, muscular, and it showed. Popular lore describes him as Rambo with a guitar, a defender of American values, a big iron-clad guy who loves the flag and also has buns of steel. It was as if the 1980s and its obsession with physical fitness had eaten him alive. It chewed up his lyrics like wafers, turning them into crumbs, then putting them back together as it pleased. That's the only way—with the photographs of Springsteen sleeveless with sweaty biceps, a handkerchief on his head, and the chorus of *Born in the U.S.A.* in the background— that everything can be misunderstood. Maybe Springsteen won't ever again be in the spotlight like he was back then. Even the single for "Dancing in the Dark" got a video directed by Brian De Palma, fresh off the smash success of *Scarface*. In that era, just being around him or entering into his orbit is all it took to be shot from his springboard into stardom. So much so that her appearance in that video launched the career of Courtney Cox. In any case, the entire album is full of sounds that were everywhere at the time, making it easily comprehensible to just about anyone. He'd embraced the sound of the era, to the degree that even those who don't necessarily listen to rock, like it. Just think of the beginning of "Born in the U.S.A.," which is a riff, but played on the keyboard. There's no electric guitar: that comes much later, when the dancing has already begun. And "Dancing in the Dark" isn't just a hit single; it's the biggest concession Springsteen has ever made to the "music heard out and about" (e.g., new wave, electropop, you could almost say "trendy," except that "trendy" is a contradiction in terms when applied to Springsteen). But that's what it is. Complete with Courtney Cox in the video, her hair done like so many other American girls who had fallen for the "second British Invasion" (i.e., new wave imported from England). She wasn't a rocker, and it showed.

97 *Springsteen with the American flag behind him.*

Success of the sort doesn't come without consequences, of course. Steve Van Zandt left the E Street Band to start his own personal project, a group called Disciples of Soul. It wasn't so much a breakup (even if legend has it that Landau, after having chased Appel off, didn't want anyone else at Springsteen's side) as Van Zandt being uncomfortable with how big they'd gotten. To him, two million album copies and sold-out concerts all over the USA was more than enough. In short, Van Zandt is the personification of the numerous traditional forces in Springsteen's life. Remaining tied to the same people that he started out with, remaining tied to the same places and mythology instead of ending up living entirely in another context (that of celebrities and other people with padded wallets), Springsteen still has a few people around him who keep his feet firmly on the ground, constantly reminding him that he came from somewhere else.

Plus, in that moment, something else happened that likely no one noticed. In fact, it wouldn't have seemed important at the time, but it would be fundamental later on: at the same time that Van Zandt left the band, a new back-up singer joined: Patti Scialfa.

98-99 Steve "Little Steven" Van Zandt and Bruce Springsteen during an interview at WQXI Radio in Atlanta, Georgia, on March 27, 1976.

1985

It was a time of change that ushered in a massive milestone: the Boss bought a house, and he bought it in California. He had a contract with the label for just over ten years, and his popularity had been on the rise for just under ten years. It was only then that he felt the desire to put down roots. He even had a bodyguard. It was all part of his new status, a world-famous star. At that point, the transition from a guy from Jersey to a showbiz star with a mansion in California was complete. Or, better yet, there was just one small thing missing, a small thing that happened soon: getting married to Julianne Phillips, a twenty-four-year-old model he had met backstage at one of his concerts. As always, anything important in his life either happens on stage or as a result of a concert itself, whether backstage or somehow linked to a tour. This time, it was the mega-tour for *Born in the U.S.A.* (so big that his London dates attracted members of the Royal Family and the ones in Dublin caused a riot in which barriers were trampled, stopping the show). Springsteen and Phillips got married in Oregon, in front of the fifty-three guests in attendance. Among the invitees was Patti Scialfa, though she didn't go: already in love, she stayed home to record her solo album, full of sad songs. Sales were pitiful, and her defeat was total.

Everything changed. Springsteen went to California, he had a bodyguard, and he married a model, Julianne Philips.

100 *Bruce Springsteen and his then-wife Julianne Philips at London's Heathrow Airport, 1985.*

1 9 8 8

102 *The stars of the Human Rights Now! tour, a series of benefit concerts for Amnesty International. Youssou N'Dour, Peter Gabriel, Bruce Springsteen, Tracy Chapman, and Sting at Wembley Stadium, September 2, 1988.*

103 *The cover of Live 1975-85 by Springsteen and the E Street Band.*

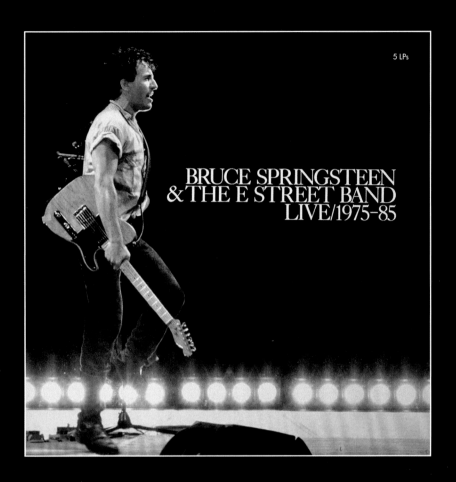

5 LPs

BRUCE SPRINGSTEEN
& THE E STREET BAND
LIVE/1975-85

So, since 1985, Springsteen's public image had been split in two, moving on parallel tracks. On the one hand, he's the most famous white musician in the world. On the other, he's got intense, frequent humanitarian commitments on stages around the world. While he refused to participate in music awards, he accepted the invite to take part in Quincy Jones and Michael Jackson's We Are the World project, followed by Artists United Against Apartheid organized by Steve Van Zandt. He played in Freehold to support the ex-employees of a closed factory, and "My Hometown" became the symbolic track of that movement. He played with Neil Young at the Bridge School Benefit, and at Jersey Artists for Mankind with a full New Jersey lineup. Then, over the following years, he played twenty dates for Amnesty International with Peter Gabriel, Tracy Chapman, Youssou N'Dour, and Sting (who he would become close friends with), ending the tour with a concert in Buenos Aires released as a live EP titled *Chimes of Freedom*, named after the Dylan cover that everyone performed at the end of the concerts.

Moreover, as a corollary to the end of an era, the famous live compilation album came out, the first official live disc after hundreds of bootlegs. *Bruce Springsteen & the E Street Band Live 1975-85* immediately topped the charts. Three million copies sold immediately, and a total of 13 million at the end of the decade, one of the best-selling live albums of all time and the first box set to come in at number one on the US best-selling albums chart.

BRUCE SPRINGS

TUNNEL OF L

One era had come to an end in some way, and another had started. The next studio album, in 1986, was *Tunnel of Love*. It was drastically different, more somber and elegant, without the stable support of the E Street Band. It's a solo album in which the musicians of the backing band appear in no particular order, with the addition of his old friend Nils Lofgren. It's an album that contains a series of more intimate, personal songs made of passion and more delicate feelings, certainly not the big rock explosions that Springsteen loved to celebrate. Like the name implies, *Tunnel Of Love* is about love, crafted from simple, time-honored ballads, an album that tells the stories of an inconsequential, everyday life in an America far from the problems of the world, an America that's fantastic and romantic, at the center of a universe in which "spare parts and broken hearts keep the world turnin' around," like Springsteen sings in "Spare Parts." It's a world in which feelings are still what pull the strings of life, in which dreams are still united with respite, but in which the "rock 'n' roll hero" seems to have been swapped out for a father at the head of the household. Nothing is new in terms of the songs' structure. Springsteen repeats a single great standard in his immense oeuvre, and he remains true to that standard on this album too. What's surprising, if anything, is the incredible capacity for renewal that he manages to express through a plot that is substantially always the same, but which always sounds new. The only truly memorable songs are the title track, destined to become a major hit and a classic in the Springsteen repertoire; the wonderful "Brilliant Disguise"; the moving "Walk Like a Man"; and "Tougher Than the Rest" and "One Step Up." But it's clear that Springsteen has headed down a different path. He's no longer Springsteen the prisoner of rock standing atop a pile of amps. Definitely not. He's the Springsteen that sings of emotional hardship.

His relationship with Julianne Phillips wasn't going very well, and no one around him was surprised. After all, the two of them never had anything in common. She was from a good family and didn't love rock 'n' roll; he came from New Jersey and rock was all he had. The unbridgeable cultural gap and mismatched social backgrounds led to the end of the marriage and a rather bloody divorce. Springsteen told his lawyers not to fight back, and Phillips got what she asked for, $20 million. There was little to negotiate and quibble over, in part because (despite the couple being broken up and Springsteen no longer wearing his wedding ring), without saying anything to anyone, he started openly dating Scialfa. Phillips even caught them snuggled up on a private plane together. Plus, while in Rome for a concert, Springsteen was photographed on the terrace of his hotel room with Scialfa. By then, not only did the entire band and Phillips know, but the entire world knew too. A communiqué making the separation official was immediately released.

HIS MARRIAGE WAS IN SHAMBLES. AND PATTI SCIALFA BECAME HIS NEW, AND DEFINITIVE, TRUE LOVE.

All that, in a certain sense, had already been explained on *Tunnel of Love*. But, as always, it was on tour that people truly learned where he was in his life, what his true desires were, and what was changing. Excitement was no longer the ruling element at his concerts in 1988; they were a bit less stadium and a bit more intimate. They had a rhythm-and-blues spirit, and even his live repertoire shrank, no longer marathons in their length. Last, but not least, while on stage, Springsteen increasingly began to play duets with his favorite backup singer, his "red-haired revolution: flaming beauty, Queen of my heart, waitress, street busker, child of some privilege, hard-time Jersey Girl, great songwriter, nineteen-year New Yorker, one of the loveliest voices I've ever heard, smart, tough, and fragile." Once the tour was over, the two began living together and work began on an album that was even more intimate than *Tunnel of Love: Human Touch*.

107 *Patti Scialfa on stage with Bruce Springsteen at Wembley Stadium in London, June 30, 1988.*

The incredible series of concerts benefiting humanitarian, social, and political causes included, at a certain point, a date in East Germany. There were 300,000 people in the audience. Organizing it was the Socialist Party, hoping it would be a tool to subdue the revolting young people, but it ended up having the exact opposite effect. Instead of calming the souls that were boiling over (the same ones that got the Wall torn down one year later), that concert only inflamed their yearning for freedom and music from the West.

But the Berlin Wall wasn't the only thing to crumble in 1989. Another symbol that seemed insurmountable also met its end that year: on September 23 (just two months before the Berlin Wall fell), on a stage, of course, that of McLoone's in Sea Bright, New Jersey, a sweaty, drunk-as-a-skunk Springsteen turned forty. There with him, almost all the members of the E Street Band were equally up to their eyeballs in alcohol. They all knew that their collaborations over the past few years hadn't been as solid or consistent as in the past, and they were probably all aware of the fact that the band would soon be broken up, after twenty years together.

108-109 *Bruce Springsteen fans holding up the* Tunnel of Love *tour poster in 1987, waiting for the concert to begin.*

110 *Bruce Springsteen holding his son, Evan James, in 1991.*

Closing out the year, Scialfa got pregnant.

Douglas Springsteen wasn't exactly a man to make big, heartfelt speeches. He was the type of American who could hold a lot of alcohol, and words, inside; a father with a lot of ideas of what his son should have been, ideas that his son Bruce had totally betrayed. He was the opposite of what his father had wanted, which is why the two had a hard time getting along. Just before the baby was born, at 11 am, there was a knock on the door of Bruce's home in Los Angeles. It was his father. He had driven all the way from New Jersey, without saying a word to anyone. Despite it being before noon, father and son sat in the kitchen and drank a beer. As Bruce tells it, what happened was the closest that Douglas ever came to saying he was sorry. There in the kitchen, he said: "You've been very good to us," adding: "I haven't been very good to you." He didn't say anything else, but the message was clear. Now that Bruce was about to become a father, Douglas wanted to break the chain of fatherly sins that had been passed down through the generations; he didn't want Bruce to make the same mistakes with his own child that he'd had to endure. Calling this moment "cardinal" would be an understatement.

Bruce Springsteen's first son, Evan James, was born in 1990, and he brought a lot of changes to his father's life. Springsteen—the same person who never stopped to rest between 1973 and 1985, the musician of giant tours, the one for whom nothing serious happened if it didn't happen at a concert, and who had begun to meditate upon a more normal existence—officially became a family man. Between 1990 and 1992, he rarely left home.

He spent almost all his time with his wife and son, but he also reconnected with many people from his past (not only his parents), including his sister. So, not only did the new family in front of him become central in his life, but also the one behind him. In 1991, he got married in Santa Monica, California. For the second time. Unlike his first marriage, however, those who know him say that this time he was truly happy and in a good place.

So, he rarely left his home in

From 1990 to 1992, the tireless Boss decided to rest. And break up the E Street Band.

Beverly Hills for that first year. And the few times he made public appearances, they were for various benefit events: two at the Christic Institute of Los Angeles, where he played an acoustic set with old and new songs. He kept going to his therapist; but now that he'd found a sort of normal life, or the closest thing to a normal life that an international rock star can have, he didn't want to let go. Finally, for the first time in forty years, he got some rest. The decade ahead of him would be the first one in which, along with new albums, he mainly put out compilations made up of previously unheard, but old and live, tracks. His discographic image itself had changed. The Nineties was to be his decade enjoying the life of a great musician who had carved a notch in the history of rock, and thus had a past to celebrate, while in the present he tried to take relatively new paths with little success. After all, he didn't want to repeat himself; that's what "best-of" albums are for. Plus, he had just broken up the E Street Band.

Not that he wasn't working. He was, just slowly and at his own pace. In all of 1990, he recorded just one song, "My Lover Man," and after three years of practically having disappeared, comparisons began with great artists who, at a certain point in life, decide not to show their face in public again.

When the three-year hiatus ended, Springsteen had written enough tracks to fill two albums.

The studio sessions to record the new work all took place on the East Coast, spanning nineteen months between September 1989 and March 1991. Lots of different artists appeared with him, some of whom were famous session musicians, two of whom had even worked on Zucchero's *Rispetto*, that is, the duo made up of Springsteen's longtime friend, David Sancious, and his partner in crime, Randy Jackson, or superstar Jeff Porcaro. Springsteen didn't want a real, true band, and the only member of the old family to make it through the revolution was Roy Bittan, who also lived in California. Instead of falling into oblivion, he played a central role. In the various months in the recording studio, they cut thirty tracks and the album was ready for release by early 1991. But Springsteen had second thoughts, and began writing new material. A year went by, and in the end it all led to two different yet contemporary albums that are in some ways an exact snapshot of the two forces that gripped him at that time. One is *Human Touch*, which seems to be classic Springsteen, radio-ready music with a big sound. The other, *Lucky Town*, is much more pared down and candid.

112 and 113 *This page: the cover of* Human Touch; *opposite: the cover of* Lucky Town. *Both albums were released at the same time, in 1992.*

114-115, 116, 117, and 118 *Bruce Springsteen during the* Born in the U.S.A. *tour, 1984.*

Neither was quite what people were expecting. Especially because Springsteen's solo sound wasn't that of the E Street Band: everything was too clean and polished, over-produced and with very little to grasp onto emotionally. They're albums that won't make much of an impact on the life of the listener, a big change for fans who were used to listening to Springsteen precisely for his ability to touch the human soul, deep down. They're albums by an American rock professional, nothing more. Very few people bought both albums, and they wound up second and third on the album sales charts, selling 1.5 million copies, half of *Tunnel of Love*, and a tenth of *Born in the U.S.A.* Overall, it can be estimated that the new Springsteen lost 66% of the audience he'd had in the 1980s, at his peak. But at the time, he didn't seem to care much. Moreover, it was also what Van Zandt had predicted would happen when the E Street Band broke up.

1 9 9 2

For the first time, even the press criticized the albums, or, at the very least, was divided into two camps. And in another first, his concerts didn't all sell out (once again, exactly what Van Zandt had said, all sold out in the US, but not necessarily abroad). It was the first time that

band was all new and, while it was perhaps perfectly tuned for his new songs, it was entirely unsuited for the old repertoire, which in fact was a very small part of his concerts at the time.

The only thing that didn't change was his participation

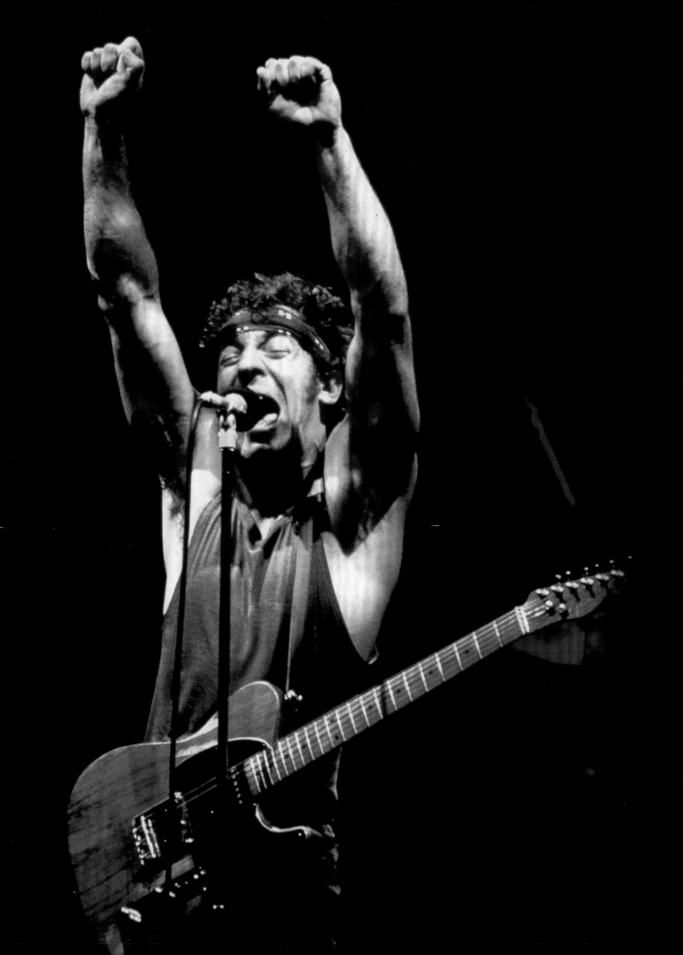

THE NINETIES
WRAPPED UP A
LEGENDARY ERA.

THE CONCERTS WERE "TOUR DE FORCE" THAT LASTED HOURS, A BLEND OF ECSTASY AND PASSION, DREAMS AND ROCK 'N' ROLL.

120 *Springsteen and singer Patti Scialfa, together on stage at Giants Stadium, New Jersey, August 22, 1985, on the* Born in the U.S.A. *tour.*

121 *Springsteen and his guitar on the* Born in the U.S.A. *tour.*

122 and 123 *Two pictures taken during the final concert of the Born in the U.S.A. tour, October 2, 1985, in Los Angeles, California.*

4

1992–2012
FROM CRISIS
TO REBIRTH

THE END OF A MILLENNIUM,
THE BEGINNING
OF A NEW LIFE

Thus began the long period of Springsteen the solo artist, no longer part of a band. It may seem odd, considering everything he'd done in the previous twenty years; but in reality, the flip side of the enthusiasm, energy, humanity, and desire to be in contact with others was depression that just wouldn't quit. That included the extreme mood swings that he had always suffered from. Springsteen could be truly awful. With everyone. Seeing his therapist was increasingly necessary. He put a spotlight on his past traumas and tried to understand them, but that didn't free him from those mood swings. In his darkest moments, he would prove to have enviable stability, only to nosedive when he was at a peak. At times, all it took was for a memory to bubble up at the wrong instant. At a certain point, starting in 2003, he even started taking antidepressants. But it wasn't just that. Like many other incredibly famous, successful people, he had an overblown self-image. He was a narcissist for sure, but on a truly profound level and, once again, in some way he was the result of his Catholic upbringing. Springsteen held the deep-rooted belief that he had the ability to change people's lives. In his words, he believed he was "the guardian of the emotions of the memories of everyone who came to see him in concert."

> **Springsteen began a path of therapy and "solitude," without the band, but with his ghosts.**

And maybe he was right. He and the E Street Band had one specific job and one precise role to fulfill in that regard. At least when they were together. Now that he was a solo artist and a dedicated family man, writing new albums made way for other endeavors. The most resounding of them was the song he wrote for *Philadelphia*, directed by Jonathan Demme. It's a beautiful title track, just keys and voice, no guitar, sung in first person, with lyrics that go straight to the heart as they talk about America and the world. And, like the film, of course, it was focused on AIDS and its consequences. It was a success, just like everything else the film touched. Profit, sales, and Oscars for all, including Springsteen. It was 1994, and it was the first time that a rock star had won the award for the best original song. The song's video was also directed by Demme, who had an entirely unique sense of music, and he included a technique that had already been tested out for the video of "Brilliant Disguise," that is, Springsteen's voice in the video was recorded live. It isn't the audio track from the album. Springsteen is actually singing in the images that were used for the video, recorded with a hidden microphone. Singing on the streets of Philadelphia.

That same year, Springsteen's second son Sam Ryan was born, which only intensified his desire to stay home and pushed the label to release compilation albums that were absolute victories. Springsteen was so close to his sons that, if he promised to take them to see *Beauty and the Beast*, he was ready to interrupt a recording session with the E Street Band to keep his promise. His priorities had completely changed.

126 *A portrait of Springsteen in 1995.*

128 *Springsteen with his Oscar, during the 66th Academy Awards held at the Dorothy Chandler Pavilion in Los Angeles, California on March 21, 1994. "Streets of Philadelphia," from* Philadelphia *directed by Jonathan Demme, won Best Original Song.*

129 *The cover of* The Ghost of Tom Joad, *1995.*

Springsteen slowly realized that the street he had once headed down wasn't the right one. He understood that the popular sentiment he had captured with *Human Touch* and *Lucky Town* was very similar to indifference. For another year, he tried to write songs in the wake of the three previous albums. Then, seeing that nothing stuck, he stopped. The band getting back together came via a concert in 1995 at Tramps in New York, but it solidified mainly for the recording of a few unreleased tracks, the kind that would boost sales for the first major compilation of Springsteen's hits. The event had the makings of something legendary, even if the band had only been broken up for seven years. And as such, *that* recording became so symbolic that it had to be celebrated, resulting in a documentary titled *Blood Brothers.* They may indeed be blood brothers, but the Boss and his band once again took different roads heading in different directions immediately after. "I had one song left over from the project. It was a rock song I'd been writing for the band but couldn't complete," he remembered. That song was "The Ghost of Tom Joad," and Springsteen used it to re-focus on himself, his needs, his relationship with writing, with important topics, with history, and with life, pushing him to make yet another solo album, with an acoustic guitar and nothing more: *The Ghost of Tom Joad,* of course. The feel of it was as far as you could get from the intensity of the band. It was inspired by *The Grapes of Wrath* by John Steinbeck (and obviously the film by John Ford too), and also by *Journey to*

1995

Nowhere: The Saga of the New Underclass, a book that earned Dale Maharidge a Pulitzer Prize. Once again it was folk, not the kind of music that sells, but the kind that wins a Grammy for best folk album. That's the exact kind of phase it was, the one in which more accolades come from critics, peers, the industry, and label execs than from fans. And he was still playing live. *The Ghost of Tom Joad* got its big world tour, with 132 concerts in eighteen months of travel (but not before having played at Frank Sinatra's 80th birthday concert, in which he gave a touching speech before launching into "Angel Eyes").

It was a tour without a band, the first time since the 1970s that Springsteen got on the stage alone, with a guitar and a harmonica. The setlist even included a new version of *Born in the U.S.A.*, which he'd adjusted the tone of, musically speaking, muting its ode-like characteristics to make it so that everything contrasted less with the lyrics. It's a version that can't be misunderstood. It's the Springsteen who covers his own song, not the one going on the attack; and moreover, they weren't exactly the kind of concerts that got him new fans. That which took place on stage on that tour was a different kind of liturgy. "In that solitary setting, where just one voice and one guitar dominated in the perfect silence, previously unknown nuances can be appreciated. There's no marvelous uproar or the overflowing energy of his usual concerts, but a suspended, electric tension, where every word is as heavy as lead, and he burns the veils of the unsettled conscience of the new America. So, he renewed the

In 1997 in Stockholm, he received the
"NOBEL PRIZE FOR MUSIC,"
the Polar Prize, in front of the Swedish royals

entirely American miracle of the wandering minstrel, of the so-called hobo that roams the nation near and far to sing to people, to tell tales and stitch up the sense of identity of a population born of voyage and cross-pollination. Almost an antidote, a natural antibody created by American culture every time one strays from the righteous path," wrote Gino Castaldo.

It's thus no surprise that the applause coming from the industry and the intellectual world was the loudest. And in 1997, Springsteen was awarded the "Nobel Prize of music," the Polar Music Prize, given by the Swedish royal family in Stockholm. After that, he finally closed out the long *Ghost of Tom Joad* tour, playing it for the wife of John Steinbeck.

131 *A moment on stage at the Wiltern Theater in Los Angeles, during the* Ghost of Tom Joad *tour.*

While new songs and albums came in a steady stream in the 1970s and 1980s, like water from the tap, things were different now. Truly new releases were a rarity in a sea of compilations, classic hits, and old songs that had previously only existed in a vault somewhere. All this came at the end of the decade, in a series of crucial changes that, not by chance, were concentrated in a few years, and whose discographic emblem would be *Tracks:* a monstrous four-album box set with sixty-six tracks, almost all of them unreleased, plus a few B-sides and other songs recorded over the previous twenty-seven years. It came out in 1998, the same year that Springsteen left California and returned to New Jersey. It's almost as if *Tracks* closed out that era and allegorically arrived the same year that Springsteen's father died. The box set contains songs from some of

In 1998, he went back to New Jersey, where he began a new phase of his life and re-formed the E Street Band.

the darkest and some of the brightest moments of his career, songs that had been set aside, and music with which to make peace and finally release. Despite not containing any big hits, it was the compilation to end all compilations, at the end of a decade of compilations. It was the putting in order and resolution of the musical path of Bruce Springsteen, and the start of another. Indeed, the *Tracks* tour reunited him

and the E Street Band. And, even though "My Love Will Not Let You Down" and "Lift Me Up" were written and composed between 1998 and 1999 for John Sayles (a friend and director of many music videos) for his film *Limbo*, years later Springsteen himself looked with a bit of regret at this decade, the one in which he admits to having worked very little and certainly didn't come up with his best work.

All that was about to end, however, because things soon returned to their frenetic pace again. After *Tracks*, there were more tracks. That is, *18 Tracks*, a collection of singles that hadn't yet appeared on other compilations, and the announcement of a tour with the E Street Band that marked the return of loud, noisy shows again, despite ten years having passed since the last time that Springsteen went full Springsteen on stage. And not just any ten years, but ten years in which he went from his forties to his fifties. There were no guarantees that the old magic could be recreated. And yet, it was. Springsteen wasn't a pathetic old man trying to act like a teenager: quite to the contrary, he wasn't out of shape, and he found a way to give off the same energy as always, without negating the time that had passed.

His first foray into acting (though playing himself and only for a few seconds) in a movie, *High Fidelity* by Stephen Frears, and being inducted into the Rock & Roll Hall of Fame (presented by Bono) were the best possible ending to what can be called his worst era.

133 *The cover of 18 Tracks, songs recorded years prior but never released.*

The massive process of going back to the roots of his career (i.e., grand performances) began in 1999 with the rehearsals for the historic reunion of Springsteen's band after ten years apart. The rehearsals of that tour gave rise to "Land of Hope and Dreams." According to Springsteen, that track is what changed everything: it "summed up a lot of what I wanted our band to be about and renewed our pledge to our audience, to point the way forward and, once again, become a living presence in our listeners' lives." Then, after almost 130 concerts, Springsteen ended the tour in New York and, to celebrate, he wrote something new. He decided to talk about the death of Amadou Diallo, a young man who was riddled with 41 bullets shot by police officers as he put his hands in his pocket to get his wallet, an event that "underscored the danger and deadly confusion of roaming the inner-city streets in black skin that still existed in late-twentieth-century America." It's a dramatic, powerful, painful song; not a song of barricades, not a track speaking out against the police,

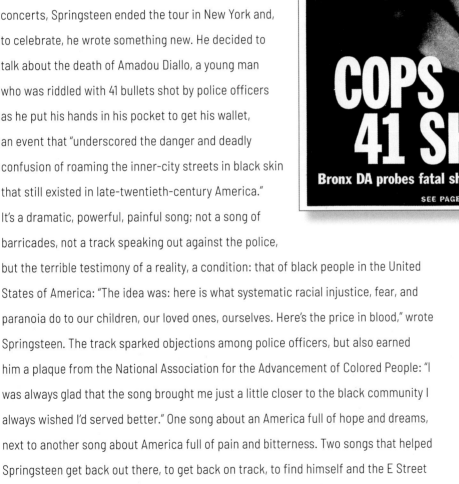

but the terrible testimony of a reality, a condition: that of black people in the United States of America: "The idea was: here is what systematic racial injustice, fear, and paranoia do to our children, our loved ones, ourselves. Here's the price in blood," wrote Springsteen. The track sparked objections among police officers, but also earned him a plaque from the National Association for the Advancement of Colored People: "I was always glad that the song brought me just a little closer to the black community I always wished I'd served better." One song about an America full of hope and dreams, next to another song about America full of pain and bitterness. Two songs that helped Springsteen get back out there, to get back on track, to find himself and the E Street Band, as demonstrated by the tour and the following live album, which kicked off the new millennium.

134 *A portrait of Springsteen from 1998.*

135 *The cover of the* Daily News, *reporting the death of Amadou Diallo, who was shot 41 times by the police.*

136 *Bruce Springsteen opening* America:
A Tribute to Heroes, *a television show organized
to raise funds after the attacks on the World
Trade Center, playing "My City of Ruins." New
York, September 21, 2001.*

2001

This rebirth culminated in the recording of a new album. It still wasn't clear what it would be and if and when it would come out, but in the meantime he started recording—with the E Street Band. It was supposed to be an album that returned to richness and fullness of sound and spirit, but history got in the way and made it one of the decade's most decisive albums in terms of popular American culture. All because one morning, September 11, 2001, before heading to the studio, as he was eating his usual breakfast cereal, Springsteen was called into the living room to watch what was happening on TV. An airplane had crashed into one of the Twin Towers. A few minutes later, another plane crashed into the other.

It was a watershed moment for Americans everywhere. But especially for those who were born, raised, and lived in New Jersey, a stone's throw from New York. Even more so for someone like Springsteen, who had founded his entire career on songs about the pure American soul and traditional values, how they're changing and, in some cases, how they've disappeared. What happened after that important event and for the following three years in Springsteen's life was an increased awareness about his role, which he ended up changing. And, as always, it all began on stage and in New Jersey. But more than anything else, it began with people. Springsteen himself has said that just a few days after the attack, while he was leaving a parking lot in Sea Bright, the driver of a car passing by shouted: "Bruce, we need you."

On September 21, a special television program was aired, called *America: A Tribute to Heroes*. It opened without words, without names, just with Bruce Springsteen, guitar in hand and harmonica around his neck, backup singers behind him, singing and playing "My City of Ruins." The track hadn't been written specifically for the event; actually, it was about a year old and talked not about New York, but about Asbury Park and its decline. But it had the right spirit and the right lyrics, a ballad that also worked as a prayer for those who are no longer here. Catholic school was but a distant memory, but those hinterlands, that upbringing, and that outlook return constantly in his work and his actions. In "My City of Ruins," he mentions empty stores, residents that wander the streets aimlessly, and then, of course, deserted churches. Everything in the name of seeking out a new source of hope from somewhere in the USA.

He wasn't just the right artist at the right time. He, Bruce Springsteen, needed that moment to take the leap forward in public perception that he had been waiting for for some time now. While in the 1990s he had been consecrated as a piece of rock history with a rainstorm of compilations, re-releases of his greatest hits, and transformations of his songs, whipped out in giant successes, marked by Oscars, Grammys, and hard work, at this point Springsteen was ready to become a symbol. A symbol of rock music, but also of a certain way of seeing America and of experiencing the status of being an American. At this point, you might not love his music, but you can't help respecting his total dedication to rock. It's impossible not to admire the way in which he filled those shoes.

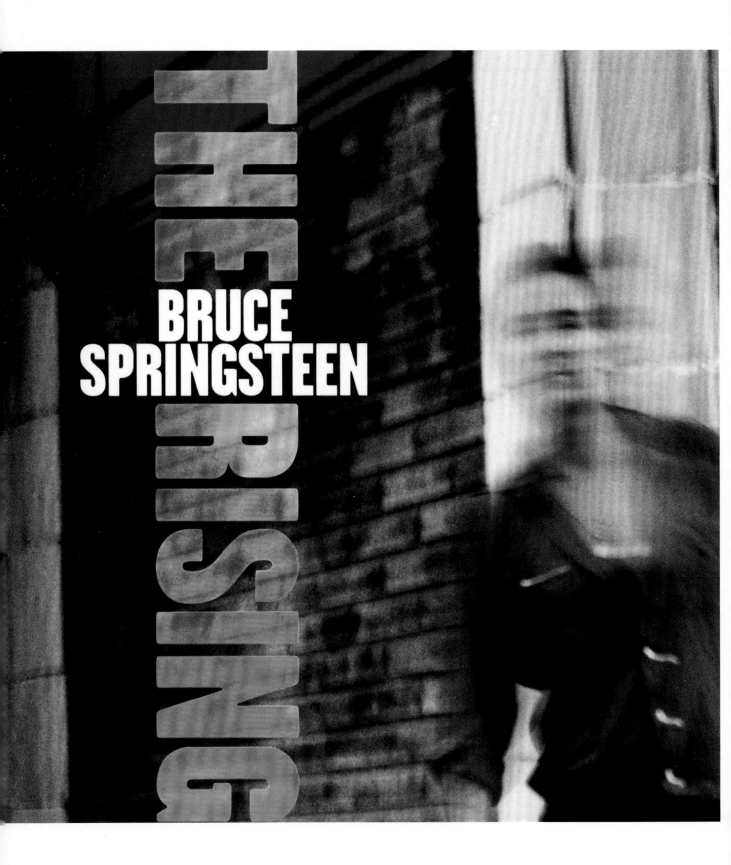

BRUCE
SPRINGSTEEN

THE RISING

Following the attacks on the World Trade Center, the *New York Times* launched the Portraits of Grief project, profiles of the victims' lives reconstructed by talking to family and friends. The goal was not only to put a face to the victims, but also to ascribe personality and depth to those who were killed. Springsteen read them all, surprised at how many times these profiles included words directed at him, at how many of those victims were his fans. The Giants fanatic, the gardening hobbyist, the tango dancer and so on, that in one case even wanted *Born in the U.S.A.* as the music played at their funeral. In another, all they did was talk about *Thunder Road,* and in another yet, they were remembered because nothing but Springsteen could be played in the car. And he called them all. He tracked them down, got their phone numbers, and called each family one by one, to comfort them, to offer his condolences. Direct phone calls, no preambles, no platitudes, just condolences and a few questions about the departed. As if to get to know them better.

That all happened between the early recording sessions pre-9/11 and the definitive ones that would shape *The Rising,* the first true rock album since the days of *Lucky Town* in 1991. Actually, given the presence of the E Street Band, it was the first truly rock 'n' roll album by Bruce Springsteen since *Born in the U.S.A.,* practically eighteen years. And so it happened that the return to that rich sound became a way to process what happened. And given its rapid release, in 2002,

it became the first piece of popular culture to reflect seriously on the attacks. Springsteen not only mourned the victims and asked what was really happening; he also included Pakistani musicians, i.e., stars from the Muslim world, and he was the first (and at that time, the only) celebrity to wonder aloud what had gone through the bombers' heads.

"The Rising" is a masterpiece that's completely, entirely, absolutely rock, with a sort of power, strength, and energy that very, very few other contemporary rock songs (or past ones, for that matter) possess.

"The Rising" is a masterpiece, a rock song about the past and rebirth.

Plus, the lyrics don't have so much as a drop of rage or resentment; there's no desire for vendetta or punishment, only the desire to rise again, to lift oneself up again, the desire for a new life amid tears and pain: "Come on up for the rising / Come on up, lay your hands in mine," he sings, with conviction, confidence, secure in the possibility that we all can live together.

138 *The cover of* The Rising, *released in 2002.*

The album contains much more than that, first and foremost the presence of the new E Street Band, an expanded version that includes Nils Lofgren, Patti Scialfa, and Soozie Tyrell, the sound of which perfectly mixes power and control. Then there are the songs: small gems and bombastic ones, such as the aforementioned "My City of Ruin," "Waitin' on a Sunny Day," "Lonesome Day," and "Countin' on a Miracle"; there's a Springsteen who is conscious of his own means, his role, his voice. Actually, he's even aware that his voice is, definitively, collective, and that the popular sentiment that he has portrayed, during a hard time for the USA, is the backbone of his artistic being.

Of course, making such an album isn't enough. If it has that sort of inspiration, that type of role, and that type of urgency, the goal is for as many people as possible to hear it. Springsteen proposed a massive marketing campaign to Columbia Records, one like never before, and the label was predictably overjoyed. The schedule was the stuff of legends, the sort undertaken by artists in peak physical shape and in the prime of life. The campaign started with periodicals, interviews in magazines, then newspapers, passing on to television both the day before the release and the day of, with the entire transmission of NBC's *Today* airing from Asbury Park, interviewing everyday people while Springsteen and the band played tracks from the album. The media tour continued on the *Late Show* (David Letterman was the host and the performance of "The Rising" was masterful); and finally a tour, whose tickets, at that point, sold out in a flash.

The Rising is Springsteen's greatest success since *Tunnel of Love,* so successful that he once again was on the cover of *Time.* But this time, the title was "Reborn in the USA," and the article described Springsteen as an artist that had reopened the discussion with the survivors of September 11. It isn't just a matter of selling lots of albums, but of having truly talked about that which needed to be talked about, with the people that needed to be talked to. Writing in *Slate*, A. O. Scott even called him "the official poet of September 11th."

No one else, by the end of 2003, had earned as much as he had with his live appearances: $115 million. And the following year, riding this wave, a new album by Patty Scialfa came out, eleven years after her last: *23rd St. Lullaby.*

141 *The cover of Time, August 4, 2002.*

TIME

Reborn
In the
USA

How BRUCE SPRINGSTEEN
reached out to 9/11 survivors and
turned America's anguish into art

But it didn't end there. By the time the promotion of *The Rising* had ended in 2003, a war had begun. The images of Baghdad being bombed pushed Springsteen even further toward social and political activism, leading him to do something he had never done before. Though he had previously responded to Reagan and said he was frightened by his being elected a few times while on stage, he had never openly supported a candidate, let alone participated in a tour to support one! But that's exactly what he did with the Vote for Change tour in 2004 in support of John Kerry. It

The war in Iraq began in 2003, and in 2004 Springsteen supported John Kerry's campaign for president.

goes without saying that, if Springsteen was going to become politically involved, it was certainly going to take place via the stage. And what a stage it was: the largest series of politically motivated concerts ever held, with the likes of REM, Pearl Jam, James Taylor, Jackson Browne, and John Fogerty alongside Springsteen. In response, the Republicans launched an unsuccessful boycott of Springsteen's music.

While on *The Rising* tour he had taken to pausing during the encore to caution the audience about that which the government was doing in the name of "national security," on this tour, for the first time, music wasn't the top priority. In fact, music became a tool to a political end. He was so invested in the election that, when all hopes were dashed and Kerry had lost to George W. Bush, the only possible remedy was to get back in the recording studio. "Let's start again," he said in a phone call to the producer of his latest albums, Brendan O'Brien, the day after Kerry's defeat.

142-143 *Bruce Springsteen and John Kerry on stage during a presidential campaign rally in 2004, at Ohio State University in Columbus on October 28, 2004.*

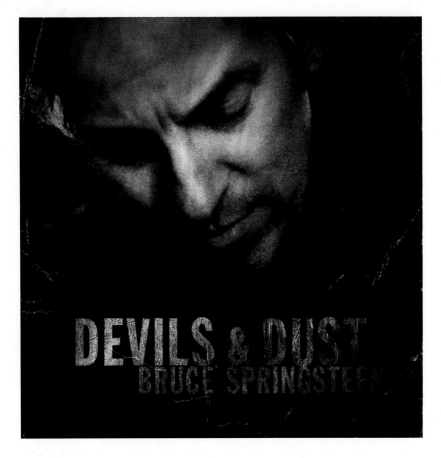

144 *The cover of* Devils & Dust, *released in 2005.*

145 *A moment from the Seeger Sessions tour, October 19, 2006.*

What resulted was *Devils & Dust*, a solo album for guitar and voice that got a tour full of instruments. Supporting Springsteen was Brendan O' Brian, not the E Street Band; the only trace of the original group was Danny Federici, appearing on just one track. Many of the songs had been written previously (the oldest being from 1991), some were from the days of *The Ghost of Tom Joad*, and the title track had already been played for years by then during sound checks. But the topic was contemporary, expressing the misgivings of a soldier stationed in Iraq. It's an anti-war track, but in a way that's anything but conventional. The concerts that followed talked about the history of rock. After the shows featuring the return of the E Street Band, after those of *The Rising* and even after those of *Vote for Change*, there were even more instruments. The spectacle and sense of entertainment ballooned. Springsteen himself didn't only play the guitar, as was customary, but instead he hopped on different instruments, changing each night depending on how things were going. Folk, myriad instruments, and even social awareness and history: slowly, a new, unique project arose, the one that would take the name *The Seeger Sessions*. Seeger, of course, is Pete Seeger, the cultural heir of Woody Guthrie, the singer of the other America, that of the people, of folk, that is hidden from the eyes of televisions or the front pages of newspapers. The America that since the 1940s had fought immense battles for civil rights, for peace, struggled against social injustice and racism. Seeger was that and much more, with his songs, his performances, concerts, protests, with a life lived on the front lines of justice and freedom. In 1997, Springsteen recorded his own version of "We Shall Overcome" as part of a tribute album to Seeger, and it was in that context that he discovered him, began to be interested in his music, changing the way he saw and understood folk.

Therefore, when he returns to rock music, he's still in sync with that America, and he consciously decides to cut an album that, as he says, was his "state-of-the nation dissent over the Iraq War and the Bush years. Still, I aimed everywhere on *Magic* for the political and the personal to meld together." The two halves finally were united.

To open the album, he chose a track that leaves no room for ambiguity, "Radio Nowhere." In it, a radio sends out signals that no one listens to. And so the album continues for its entire forty-eight minutes, twelve tracks, an LP in which rock remains the heart of its sound, and passion is at its emotional core. Passion for life, people, America, a country that he loves

but that increasingly often he doesn't recognize. So, between sweet and bitter, we listen to "Long Walk Home," the long walk for a home that makes you feel safe, "Last to Die," with those who died "for a mistake" on every street of the world, or with "Your Own Worst Enemy," where Springsteen talks about us, about fear entering our homes, which the government itself promotes. But there are brighter moments, such as the pretty "Girls in Their Summer Clothes," and moments of pain, such as that of the highly personal ghost track that ends the album, "Terry's Song." It isn't an incredible album, and there practically are no masterpieces on it. However, it certainly embodies rediscovered equilibrium. There's no anxiety about success, no need for confirmation: Springsteen simply says and does what he feels like saying and doing, and that's enough.

The tour for *Magic* was the last in which audiences could get a taste of the original lineup of the E Street Band. In 2007, while on the road, the band's longtime keyboard player Danny Federici was forced to give up the tour to seek treatment for melanoma; he came back for the show in Indianapolis in March 2008 and asked to play "Sandy." He passed away just a few days later, April 17. He had been in the band since day one, and at his funeral Springsteen played that same track, "Sandy." His death obviously meant that all concert dates from that point up to the funeral were cancelled, but because nothing in Springsteen's life exists if it doesn't exist on stage, the band was in Tampa the day after the funeral, as originally planned. That concert began with a Danny Federici tribute video and a spotlight on his empty stool behind the organ. It was all a giant celebration of his life, the true funeral wake that the band dedicated to their missing

146 *The cover of* Magic, *signed by all members of the E Street Band.*

147 *A photograph taken in Boston on November 19, 2007, with*

148 *The cover of* Working on a Dream.

149 *United States President Barack Obama and Springsteen embrace before a speech in Madison, near the Wisconsin State Capitol building, on November 5, 2012.*

In what would become a sort of tradition, Federici's son filled in for him, using his same instrument, for the recording sessions of "The Last Carnival," one of the tracks on the new album, *Working on a Dream* (2009). The title track made its worldwide debut played by Springsteen live at an Obama rally held on November 2 in Cleveland, Ohio: this time, the dream worked. Obama was elected, one of the greatest moments in American history; and one of the songs played during the inauguration event was "The Rising," as if to compensate for the letdown four years prior. And to highlight the hope that the election had been put into gear with the slogan "Yes, we can," a motto that had much in common with the entire Springsteen epic.

In any case, especially if the E Street Band was there with him, working on the dream meant softening tones, be they political or musical. One could say that *Working on a Dream* was the first knowingly "pop" album of the Boss's entire musical adventure. The nuances became more delicate, with melodies that peek out over the rhythm, all the elements of his past—rock, soul, folk—are fused in a series of songs that seem to talk also, if not mainly, to those who had never listened to Springsteen, to a mainstream audience that it was probably right to open the door to.

The resulting album is interesting, intense, calm, and deep, though again without memorable masterpieces. A few things to mention are: the initial track, "Outlaw Pete," with a new and, at that point, central quotation of Morricone, to the pretty "Queen of the Supermarket," with its simple, direct love, to the painful and already-mentioned "The Last Carnival," and a special song written for the main character of a movie, one that almost seems to have come straight from Springsteen lyrics, "The Wrestler." It's a

He won a Golden Globe with a track titled "The Wrestler," which was part of the soundtrack of the film by the same name, starring Mickey Rourke and directed by Darren Aronofsky.

film that stars Mickey Rourke in the role of a once-successful wrestler who has lost it all, an incredibly consistent American reject from a small town who is ready to die to find the glory he had always sought, directed by Darren Aronofsky. It didn't win an Oscar, but it did get a Golden Globe.

150 *Springsteen live during the halftime show of*
Super Bowl XLIII. The Arizona Cardinals played
the Pittsburgh Steelers on February 1, 2009, at
the Raymond James Stadium in Tampa, Florida.

2 0 0 9

Let's take a step back. In 2008, something else had happened: during the Super Bowl, Springsteen watched Tom Petty & the Heartbreakers play at halftime. The year before, it was the artist formerly known as Prince, and before that it was the Rolling Stones, while in 2005, Paul McCartney played. The halftime show is made up of twelve very dense, very spectacular, but also very watched minutes (usually over 100 million viewers around the globe), 12 minutes that big musicians had historically avoided. But the world had changed a lot, especially the music industry and its profits. At that time, as Tom Petty played the Super Bowl halftime show, Springsteen felt it too, and suddenly asked something he had never asked before. He picked up the telephone, called his producer, O'Brien, to ask him that question, and discover that he too was sitting before his television, also one of those 100 million spectators. He asked: "Why haven't I ever played?"

So, in 2009, between the first and second halves of the Super Bowl, Springsteen and the E Street Band appeared on the stage. They had just twelve minutes, or rather thirteen because Springsteen can't follow the rules and goes over the time limit at the only event in which everyone, truly everyone, is prohibited from going over. At that point, a man dressed as a referee gets on stage and tells him he has to go before playing even one more minute, and the last words he said before wrapping it up were a joking "I'm going to Disneyland! (the Super Bowl is held in Florida, which is also home to Disney World). But, despite the short length of the concert, it was no small thing. For an artist who had made his career and then his life a celebration of live music and the relationship with the audience, that was the biggest audience there could possibly be. For the first time, you got the impression that he was playing for everyone and not for someone. At least that's the impression other people had. Once those thirteen minutes were over, minutes in which he managed to create a short synthesis of the live show as he intends it to be when he's with the E Street Band (there was a large part of their routine, moves, tricks, and applause-underwear-excitement-evoking solutions that he had become famous for), and as he went home in record time via private jet, Springsteen wasn't sure how it had gone. For once, he failed to understand it. Everything happened so fast, and he didn't have enough time to feel the pulse of such a heterogenous audience that wasn't necessarily "his." In the days that followed, however, Springsteen, one of the most famous and beloved musicians in America, felt the effect with his own hands. Many of the people who he met complimented him or recognized him in some way precisely thanks to that performance. He truly had played for everyone.

In 2009, Springsteen played for 13 minutes (instead of 12) before 100 million people during the Super Bowl halftime show.

Perhaps as a result of such a large show, perhaps out of a desire to increasingly accommodate the wishes of the public, from that moment on, his concerts were filled with old tracks. Up until 2009, he hadn't been very inclined to revisit his career, but more inclined to play his new songs, despite the fact that, now that the Internet was a thing, his fans had more than one way and occasion to object to that decision and ask him to play his old songs. They were pressures that had always annoyed Springsteen, but which he decided to give in to, starting with the last dates of his 2009 tour, when he began performing some of his fundamental albums live from start to finish. All of *Born to Run*, all of *Darkness on the Edge of Town*, *Born in the U.S.A.*, or *The River*, or even all of *Greetings from Asbury Park, N.J.*!

Rolling Stone, which over the years had given Springsteen just about every honor, title, award, and epithet there is, named him "artist of the decade" in the late 2000s.

The second historical and stable member of the E Street Band to leave this Earth, in 2011, after Danny Federici, was Clarence Clemons, the Big Man, or, as Springsteen dubbed him when presenting him on the stage, "The Biggest Man You Ever Seen." Clemons was indeed very large, and he'd even had a chance to join a professional football team as a young man. He chose the saxophone instead. And it was a good choice, because he immediately was a hot commodity. Though he was from Virginia, he ended up in New Jersey, following bands and musicians, and it was there that he recorded an album with Norman Seldin & the Joyful Noyze.

In 2011, after Danny Federici, the E Street Band lost another member, their dear friend Clarence Clemons.

Because it was impossible to play in New Jersey around 1970 and not know Springsteen, the two had crossed paths. They sniffed each other out, they liked each other, but the first time that they could truly play together was when Clemons worked up the courage to introduce himself during an evening when Springsteen's band was playing, between sets, smashing through a door. That is, it was a night of rain and intense wind; and that, according to Clemons, caused the door to break when he opened it. But when Springsteen recounts the story, it changes a bit and turns into Clemons breaking down the door with his sheer bulk. Indeed, the band was startled and when Clemons, standing in the smashed doorway and a bit nervous because of what he was about to propose, said "I want to play with you," the only possible response to that giant man that no one had ever seen in their life was: "You can do whatever you want." They played "Spirits in the Night" and it was love at first sight. It goes without saying that, for the saxophone parts on that track and "Blinded by the Light" on *Greetings from Asbury Park, N.J.*, it was Clemons that they called. On the tour for that album, Clemons was already in the band (as was Federici) and he never left until his death on June 18, 2011, despite incredible joint problems and pain that often jeopardized his presence.

The news of his death was preceded by six days by news that he had had a stroke. Springsteen found out while

he was celebrating his 20th wedding anniversary with Scialfa in France: he hopped on the first plane to Palm Beach, as did all the other members of the band. The six days of worry were at one point brightened by a flash of wellbeing that deluded everyone into thinking that he would be able to return from that abyss. But instead, the next day, Clemons relapsed into such a state that the best option was to turn off the machinery that was keeping him alive, because "by then his soul had already left his body." When the decision was made, Springsteen grabbed his guitar and shut himself in the hospital room for three hours, playing and singing for Clemons and his family.

153 *Bruce Springsteen and Clarence Clemons, the heart of the E Street Band, on stage at Glastonbury in 2009.*

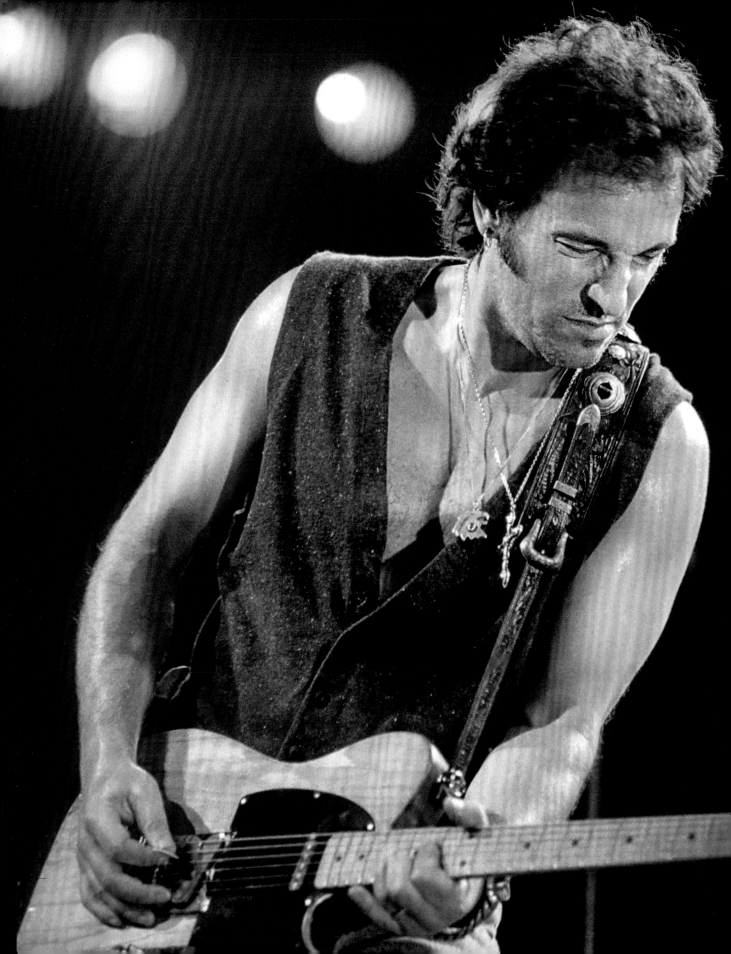

WITHOUT CLEMONS, SPRINGSTEEN IS ALONE, AMID HUNDREDS OF THOUSANDS OF PEOPLE WHO LOVE HIM.

154 and 155 *Two photographs of Springsteen playing live in Paris at the Palais Omnisport (Bercy) on June 29, 1992.*

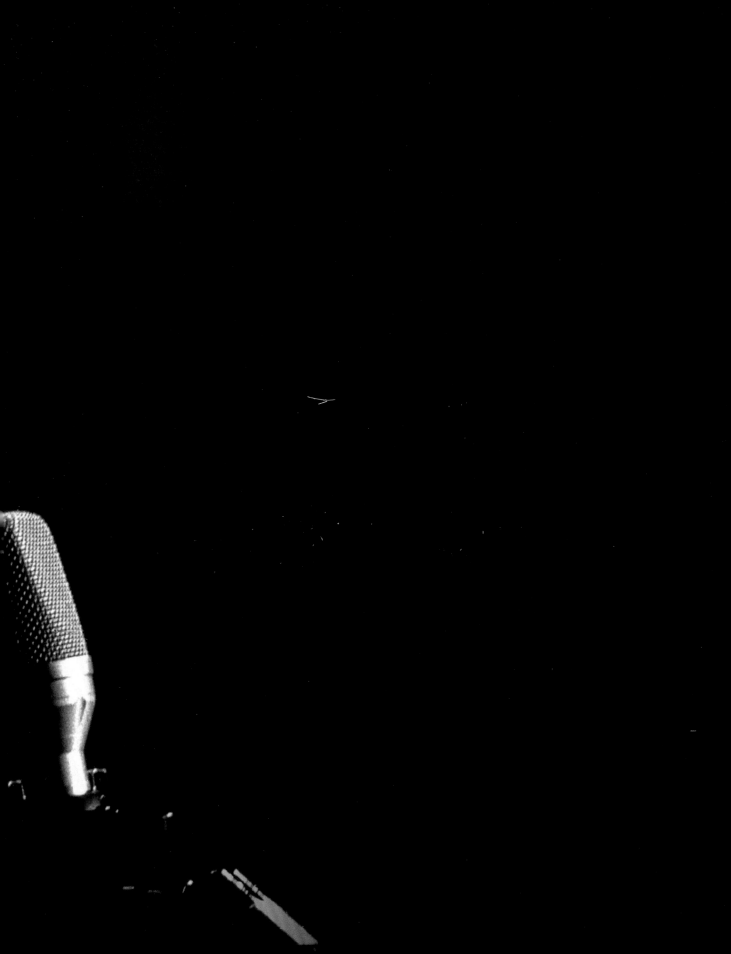

158 Max Weinberg on drums overlooking Nils Lofgren
and Bruce Springsteen during a concert.

158-159 From left: Nils Lofgren on guitar, Clarence
Clemons on saxophone, and Springsteen on guitar.

2009

160 *From left: Steve Van Zandt, Springsteen, and Patti Scialfa.*

161 *Springsteen during an exciting moment on stage at the Toyota Center in Houston, Texas, on April 8, 2009.*

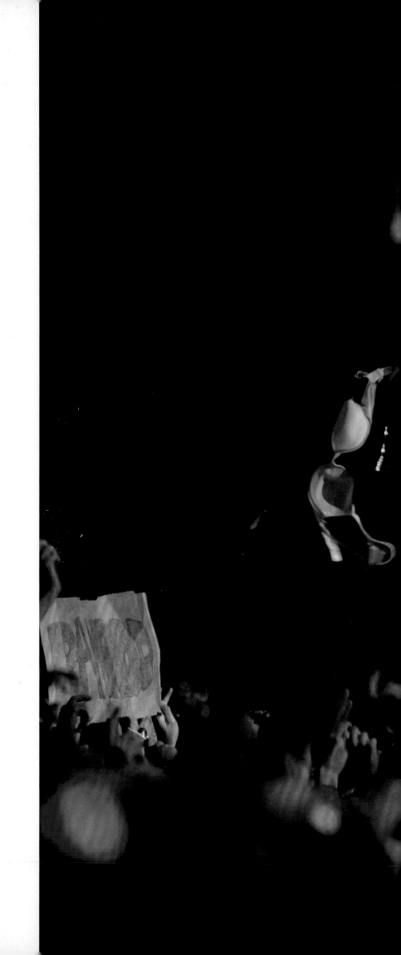

162-163 *Springsteen in 2009, surrounded by the many flags that always enliven the pit at Glastonbury.*

5

2012–2023

BIG DREAMS, BIG HOPES

THE CALL OF THE ROAD, **TRIUMPH OVER DEATH,** THE NEED TO START AGAIN

Released in 2012, the new album, titled *Wrecking Ball,* was influenced by that hard-to-bear bereavement. The music was there, the songs were put together, and one day, eating a pizza in a restaurant in Freehold, Springsteen began thinking about how the times they were living in were characterized by a distancing from America's roots, distancing from those very dynamics that were at the base

After just four months after Clemons's death, Springsteen already felt the need to get back in the studio.

of American life in the twentieth century, the one that Springsteen had always celebrated. He decided it was because many people had sought out an easier life to make money, overlooking all the rest, forgetting about the American spirit. That gave rise to "Easy Money" and the entire feel of the album. Recording began just four months after Clemons had passed, even if "Land of Hopes and Dreams," finally on an album, features a saxophone solo by the Big Man, created by assembling parts from other never-released solos recorded over the years. It wasn't an easy decision to make.

Wrecking Ball is a great, beautiful album, one of the best of Springsteen's career. Maybe it was the pain, maybe it was the crisis of the nation, maybe it was something else, but it in fact contains the best collection of Springsteen songs in years. It's an album, first of all, and not a gathering of songs. It has a spine, an atmosphere, a tone, a sense that they're complete from start to finish.

PASSING THE BATON

2012

168 *Springsteen on stage with Clemons's nephew, Jake Clemons, who passionately took his uncle's place in the E Street Band.*

And it has laudable honesty and strength. There is also rage: "After the crash of 2008, I was furious at what had been done by a handful of trading companies on Wall Street. *Wrecking Ball* was a shot of anger at the injustice that continues on and has widened with deregulation, dysfunctional regulatory agencies and capitalism gone wild at the expense of hardworking Americans." He couldn't be any clearer. But that wasn't enough. Because it's easy to see that it's all true, that Springsteen is truthful, that he doesn't talk about things that he doesn't believe in, he confesses openly and in front of everyone in *This Depression*, talking about his struggle with depression, the black hole he falls into, of the need for help that he has, first of all. It's an unbelievable laceration on his life, on the legend of the unchanging Boss, the hero of rock 'n' roll that can in fact fall: "I've been down but never this down, I've been lost but never this lost. I haven't always been strong but never felt so weak," he sings, putting his unease out there for everyone to see. His depression had arrived some time before, just after his 60th birthday in 2009, and, as Springsteen has said, "it was devastating." It wasn't short in duration, it's still there, but he hit the abyss between sixty and sixty-two years old for the first time, then again between sixty-three and sixty-four. When Springsteen talks about it in the song, he's going back to being himself. "I knew this was the music I should make now. It was my job."

But America isn't the same in people's minds; Americans are divided more than ever before and the album—despite its excellent critical reception, despite being number one on the charts (for the tenth time)—wasn't as successful and it didn't get the popular acclaim that it should have. And Springsteen knew in some way that rock was to blame: "I came to terms with the fact that in the States, the power of rock music as a vehicle for these ideas had diminished."

But the thing is that it wasn't an album of "old" rock. To the contrary, it was one of Springsteen's most aware and well-done attempts to keep his music contemporary. Even the E Street Band had been modernized, and the long list of musicians on the album didn't include Roy Bittan and Garry Tallent, while new talent had been added to the mix, first and foremost Tom Morello, the super guitarist from Rage Against the Machine becoming part of Springsteen's court. But the album does have some memorable songs, like "We Take Care of Our Own," "Jack of All Trades," "Shackled and Drawn," the wonderful "Rocky Ground," and the intense "Death to my Hometown." They were songs that became epic when played live.

On tour, the new sound and style of the expanded E Street Band was honed, and the concerts truly made an impact, despite the hole left by the Big Man. As happened after Federici's passing, the solution was in the family. Jake Clemons, Clarence's nephew who also happened to be a saxophonist, joined the band for the usual big tour, ready to take off as soon as the commitments for Obama's reelection campaign were fulfilled.

By then, Springsteen was a sixty-four-year-old musician with an incredible past and, in 2012, he ended up once again with the first-place tour in terms of the number of attendees. Mind you, at that age, most musicians are retiring. Not Springsteen. He began increasing the tour dates and duration, and even grew his audience. Because it's hard not to believe in his enthusiasm, sweat, smiles, and his desire to play for himself and for others, and "the heart-stopping, pants-dropping, house-rocking, earth-quaking, booty-shaking, Viagra-taking, love-making, le-gen-dary E-STREET-BAND!," as the Boss often riffed when presenting them. It's hard not to believe in a sixty-four-year-old man who plays for three and a half hours without stopping, singing with a voice that's strong, powerful, in tune, and absolutely enviable, going out to shake hands and hug his fans, always close to the audience, there *with* the audience, for the entire night. It's hard not to believe in his music: "Can you feel the spirit?" he'd ask the crowd before starting the show. And those

It's hard not to believe in a 64-year-old man who plays for at least three and a half hours every night, giving this soul to the audience.

who didn't "feel the spirit" at first, those who were skeptical, those who didn't have faith, at the end of the concert in all likelihood have changed their mind. Because Bruce Springsteen is the greatest rock performer alive. Because he has a mission. Like always, on this tour, Springsteen gives off the impression that he's there because he needs to be, because that's his life, his mission, not his "work." Like every concert before, he gets down from the stage, walks among the crowd, not to prove that he's a star, but for the exact opposite reason: to try to erase the distance, to once again accept the mandate that the people have assigned him for forty years now, to express hopes, dreams, and passion through his songs.

Of course, it's an illusion. Life doesn't always give us the opportunities that we want, even if we know that, deep inside, we're "born to run."

But that illusion, which has manifested itself at other concerts with other rock stars, is clear. With Springsteen, it becomes reality. Because he doesn't sing about lives that are different from ours, he doesn't tell stories that people can't identify with. His are tales of losers who want to keep playing, dreamers who, despite everything crumbling around them, don't want to stop dreaming, people who perhaps will never be wildly successful, rich or famous, but who live wonderful lives anyway.

And then there's all that's shared. Sure, he's a star. He's got money, success, and fame, but he conveys popular sentiment like very few before him and even fewer after him. And he doesn't do so on his albums; he does it at his concerts, when body and soul are at play, when he's no longer an "artist" that presents his music with mediation of the object, but one who gets on stage to touch people's hearts. If there's a contemporary word that perfectly describes Springsteen's concerts, it's "sharing." The Boss's audience shares an experience, feelings, and no one is alone. And it shows.

You don't have to like his albums; you may think, and perhaps rightly so, that the deeply creative phase of his career as a songwriter ended in the late 1980s; you can think he's old, uninteresting, repetitive, unchanging since the 1970s; but if you set foot in one of his shows and you believe that music, rock music in particular, can change your life, Springsteen is still the one to do it. With raucous energy. You don't have to love the songs he's recorded in the studio, because every time he plays them live, they're a different beast. They're alive, they're pulsating energy and intense emotion. Those songs are rock 'n' roll, which isn't so much a musical genre but a way of doing things, and Springsteen is more familiar, better versed in that way of doing things than anyone else. Only the deaf refuse to listen, only the blind can't see. Everyone else, those who pack venues on every tour date, at the end of each exhausting, never-ending concert, leaves dead-tired, but happy. Happy. Can you think of anyone else who can produce happiness in three and a half, maybe even four hours of rock 'n' roll?

success of *Wrecking Ball*, *High Hopes* objectively doesn't hold a candle. But, thanks to Morello's collaboration on eight out of twelve tracks, there are elements of an updated sound and the style, starting from the fact that since *The Rising*, Springsteen hadn't ever put out a fully rock album like this one, supported by the E Street Band, including Federici and Clemons, because some of the tracks were first recorded a decade prior. The sound and approach to the songs is heterogeneous, from the title track, "High Hopes," a song by the Havalinas that Springsteen had already cut and released on an EP in 1996, revisited on the new album with Morello's guitar at the forefront. Then there's "Harry's Place," which let Morello duet virtually with Clemons's sax, and also a high point of the album,

High Hopes came out in 2014, and it was the first time in Springsteen's career that he put out an album that wasn't entirely original, but only covers and unreleased recordings of old songs. That means that many tracks still feature Federici and Clemons. The former had passed six years before; the latter, three. Apparently, it's a "minor" album, with few new tracks, and plenty of songs from the past that have been picked up again, reworked, and recreated with the help of Morello and the "new" band, plus four cover songs. But is it really a "minor" album? Considering the

"High hopes" gave life to an album with Tom Morello appearing on guitar.

the beautiful "41 Shots," a version of the song with the passionate, anguished emotion of Morello on guitar. One of the strongest tracks on the album is the new version of "The Ghost of Tom Joad," an inevitable link between Morello and Springsteen due to its subject matter and expressive power. Here, the Rage Against the Machine guitarist takes over, sings a verse, wails on his guitar backed by the E Street Band, in a less captivating version than the original, but one that's absolutely explosive. On up to the surprising cover of Suicide's "Dream Baby Dream," a shining example of how Springsteen is able to reinterpret the entire history of rock music and make it his own.

It isn't the only moment in which he's looked to the past before looking to the future. In 2015, *The Ties That*

Bind: The River Collection came out. It contains four CDs with various unpublished tracks, three DVDs (or Blu-Rays), and a 148-page book. It was the thirty-fifth anniversary of the release of The River, and it kicked off a tour that was anything but conservative. Instead, it was a celebration of their way of understanding music, an even more extreme one in which Springsteen and the E Street Band played the longest concert of their career: four hours and four minutes. And we aren't talking about a handful of dates either, but the most successful tour of 2016. Again. At sixty-seven years old.

The only way to follow up such a tour is to do the exact opposite. So, in 2017, Springsteen played on Broadway, at the Walter Kerr Theatre, for eight weeks. Just 970 seats, far less than the 80,000 of his more hardcore shows, and "the smallest place I've played in the last forty years," he'd say. They were supposed to be spread over four weeks, but in the end, he played 236 shows. It's a performance composed of songs, sure, but mainly of conversations, speeches, and monologues on the career and world vision of Bruce Springsteen. An album and a Netflix special were made from it, both titled Springsteen on Broadway. "I've never worked for more than five days in a row in my life. Until now," is how it begins. That all happened in winter. In summer, the affair was repeated, but this time at the St. James Theatre, for another thirty-one shows.

For five nights a week, the "prisoner of rock 'n' roll" had found a steady job, filling the Walter Kerr Theatre, not so much with a concert, but with a highly theatrical performance with a relatively standardized set list and lots of talking. He put out his autobiography, and the script to

the show was his life, without smoke and mirrors, fifteen tracks, from "Growin' Up" to "Born to Run," following in the wake of his autobiography. Born to Run was the obvious but unavoidable title. The show was overpowering, very personal and intimate, light years from the Springsteen of arenas and stadiums, from rock 'n' roll, the overwhelming energy of the band, and the "mission" of making people happy for three hours.

172 The cover of High Hopes.

173 The marquee of the Walter Kerr Theatre on August 10, 2017, which reads "Springsteen on Broadway."

Instead, it was just him, with his limits, faults, and gifts, a unique, incredibly intimate event in which he truly opened up to the audience. But the show also had a few big problems, mainly the nightly repetition of an essentially pre-written script, from which the Boss deviated very, very little. Everything that was improvisation, enthusiasm, and truth in the moment during his concerts became predetermined and static, and, after a while, recited. Fake, say his more inflexible fans. Springsteen responded, saying that he was doing so as a form of respect for those who can come to just one show, because it wouldn't be right if each spectator got more or less than another. Then, another problem that can't be understated: the excessively high price of the tickets, which often reached numbers that were absolutely beyond reason in the resale market. It isn't exactly the right choice for the hero of "the working class." But, to compensate, once the show cycle ends, it can be streamed on Netflix, and an album was released. In reality, *Springsteen on Broadway* was something no one had seen before. It was like watching Elvis talking about himself, in first person, while singing his songs. It's like going out one night with Bob Dylan or Lennon and McCartney, or even Johnny Rotten, and hearing not their most obvious, most famous stories, but their more intimate, deepest truth. Despite being repetitive, the show was unique and authentic, with Springsteen's fragility put front and center, shining a new light on his entire past, all of his songs. It's a performance in which, talking about himself to others, Springsteen came to terms with himself, doing so (like every important event in his life) from the stage.

2017

174-175 *Springsteen during the last round of applause before the curtain fell at the Walter Kerr Theatre in New York, on December 15, 2018, for the final show of* Springsteen on Broadway.

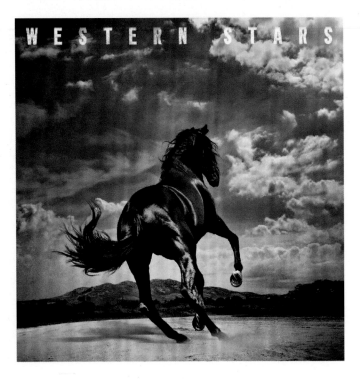

For a new album with new songs, his fans had to wait until 2019. *Western Stars* was presented at the Festival of Toronto, along with a film of the same title co-directed by Springsteen and Thom Zimny. It isn't a work of fiction, but a recording of a show in which Springsteen and his band play the tracks on the album before a live audience.

There are many ways to be Bruce Springsteen. The rock 'n' roll prophet, the urban singer-songwriter, the minstrel from the heartland, the hard rocker from the

176 *The cover of the album* Western Stars.

177 *A still taken from the film* Western Stars, *directed by Springsteen and Thom Zimny in 2018.*

outskirts, the spotless, fearless front man, the melancholy folk singer; there's the Springsteen who resists evil and the Springsteen who makes people cry softly, and the Springsteen that pushes you to yell at the top of your lungs, or the one that caresses your sadness. Anyone who thinks of Springsteen as a monolith doesn't truly know him. And anyone who thinks he's infallible, more than anything else, hasn't seen the weakness, insecurity, and uncertainty that have followed him and left their mark on his artistic past. Sure, it seems crazy to imagine all that concealed behind his image as a rock 'n' roll hero, especially once you've seen Springsteen and the E Street Band on stage. But the truth is what's hidden between the notes of "Western Stars": at seventy years old, after all the success, applause, awards, and glory, Bruce Springsteen is still figuring out who he is. And the best Springsteen is the one that, born to run, continues to run, in every possible different direction, seeking salvation and redemption and pushing us to do the same. In the very points where his music and songs become their weakest, least interesting, and, let's be honest, their worst, is when he believes, imagines and thinks he's reached a goal and, armed with that security, "he believes it." It's the Springsteen of unforgettable albums like *Human Touch* or *Magic*, of songs that have their redeeming qualities, but don't make a mark on the soul. *Western Stars* is an album that goes straight to the heart; it came in the wake of his monumental albums, and Springsteen is right when he calls it a gem. Indeed, because it has the feel of craftsmanship, it contains (in the compositions by Springsteen and in the production by now-inseparable Ron Aniello) the delight for small details, close attention to every single note, never a special effect for its own sake, never the plot twist to make people jerk in their chairs, never a firework that makes you look up to the heavens out of wonder or a sonic boom for the final rush of emotion. No, here the watchword is "harmony." Which doesn't mean simplicity, because the only simple thing on *Western Stars* is the ultimate, definitive sense of communication with others, the use of melody as an emotional latch to open the heart of the listener, the desire, the need, or rather the overt goal to put out the flames of rage, division, separation, and argument to illuminate the desire for community and sharing, slow, attentive tranquility, the kind that we all need, or should have. The Springsteen of *Western Stars* is perfectly imperfect and doubtful. He offers no certainty, only guesses, at times optimistic, at other

times gloomy. He doesn't want to take a snapshot of reality for what it is, but rather show what it potentially could be. Cinematic imagery is evident, and Springsteen recounts stories big and small, wanting us, through the arrangements, to be able to "see them," not just hear them. The arrangements are the keystone to most of the tracks, because in some cases, the style of the composition is so Springsteenian that you can almost hear, in the background, hidden away somewhere, the E Street Band playing the same songs. But there's no need here for Little Steven or Roy "The Professor" Bittan, here it's more like Burt Bacharach, strings and orchestras come in, there's the cinemascope, technicolor, all that's lacking is surround

Springsteen tells small stories, which can be "seen" more than heard.

sound to "see" the songs. The arrangements allow the lyrics to be in line with the idea of reviving a "good" sort of pop that's empathetic, not violent; they warm the heart and, going back to what we said at the start, they make their mark on the soul. *Western Stars* is a beautiful, wonderful album that's completely unlike anything else Springsteen has ever released. There are memorable tracks, others that contain atmospheres and lyrics of note, and very, very few that are just there as filler. It's worth sitting in your car, turning on the stereo, putting the album on, and taking off. The album supported the tour, with an updated E Street Band, with three top-shelf guitarists: Little Steven, Nils Lofgren, and Tom Morello. Three generations, three sounds, three different dreams. It was the most fortunate tour in the band's history.

Even when, the following year, in 2020, the "Letter to You" single came out, announcing a new album of the same name, the track was preceded by a documentary, also titled *Letter to You*, directed by Thom Zimny on his own this time. It's yet another album influenced by the death of someone, this time George Theiss, a friend and companion since the days of the Castiles. All of *Letter to You* is infused with the theme of aging, of having regrets, and dying. It also includes, of course, tracks fished out of the archive, in this case a few songs that, consistent with Theiss's death, were from as far back as possible, from the era as close as possible to the Castiles, i.e., from 1973, just before *Greetings from Asbury Park, N.J.* was recorded.

Springsteen looks to the past so as not to get lost. He thinks, rightly in many ways, that America has lost its way. In 2016, Donald Trump became President of the United States of America, due to the way the American electoral system works (Hillary Clinton won 48% of the popular vote, while Trump got 46%). Thus began a challenging time for the US and the world, and Springsteen went through it while struggling with depression, again and a lot. When *Letter to You* came out

In 2020, after 11 years, Springsteen finally got the E Street Band back together to make a new album, the first without Clemons and Federici.

in 2020, the American public was heading to vote. "Trump won't win,"

predicted Springsteen, a Biden supporter, while the album tried to encapsulate the "unsettling times" that the US was going through. *Letter to You* came out on November 23, accompanied by a nice film, again by Thom Zimny, a collection of memories and hopes, encapsulated in new songs or songs that hadn't yet been recorded. It had been since 2009 that he hadn't recorded

an album with the E Street Band—and for that release, *Working on a Dream,* the now-deceased Clarence Clemons and Danny Federici were still with him.

Everything had changed in those eleven years, Springsteen first of all, but also the world around him and, in particular, the USA: "The country as a shining light of democracy has been destroyed by this administration," he stated. "We've abandoned our friends, made friends with dictators, and denied climate science." Even if it isn't an "angry" or political album, it was impossible for the reality outside not to creep into the songs of the most lucid, attentive artist in American music.

And, in fact, there is one track, "Rainmaker," that fully comes down on the "unsettling times" that we're living in, as Springsteen defines them. "I think I wrote *Rainmaker* when Bush was President," he's said. "I started writing it around that time, but it was much better suited to Trump. I think that's so because it talks about a demagogue; it's a song in which I try to understand what's happening, what the connection is between the demagogue and his followers, what the power dynamic is between them. It's a very interesting topic and it's a very good rock song, so I decided to put it on the album. It had been in the drawer for a while; I took it out again because I think that it's directly related to our current situation."

Trump lost the election, but the USA underwent the biggest democratic crisis in its history, with the attack on Capitol Hill. Then came the COVID-19 pandemic, immense collective fear, an invisible virus that kills like something out of a sci-fi movie, empty streets, deserted cities, people locked up at home, the exact opposite of the world that Springsteen had always sung of and celebrated. But in spite of it all, he didn't give up.

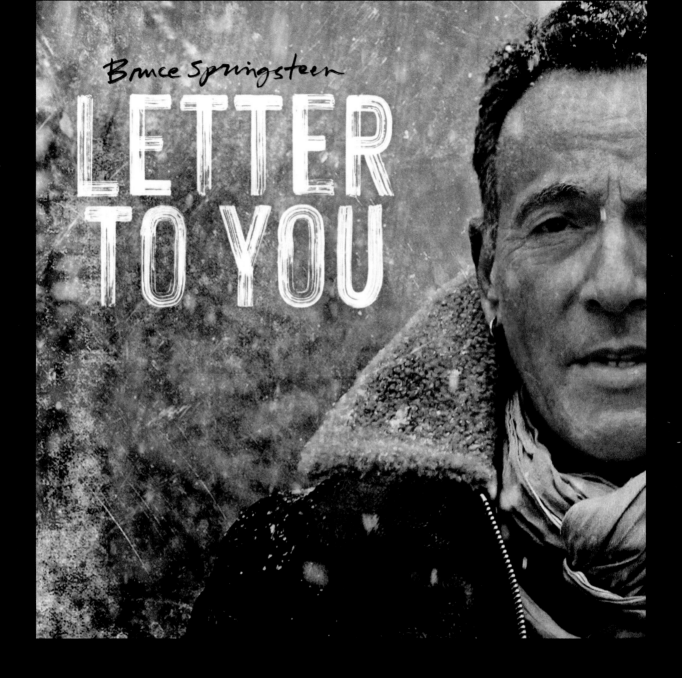

The cover of Letter to You, Springsteen's 20th album, released in 2020.

IN 2021, OBAMA AND SPRINGSTEEN RECOUNTED THEIR STORIES AND THOSE OF AMERICA IN A PODCAST AND A BOOK.

In 2021, Springsteen participated in a production for Higher Ground, the company founded by Michelle and Barack Obama, out of the White House for some time now and a content creator with a multimillion-dollar contract with Spotify. One of those productions was for *Renegades: Born in the USA,* an eight-episode podcast of just under an hour each in which Barack and Bruce discussed various topics. The idea came up after a concert held at the White House just before Obama left office. The two had spoken for the audience, and Michelle Obama had the idea of turning it into a show. It undoubtedly says something about the status of Springsteen, but also about the type of balance that exists in America between political celebrities and those in entertainment. Plus, the eight episodes were recorded at Springsteen's house, meaning that the former President had to come to him, and not vice versa.

180-181 *An image from Anthony Mason's CBS interview with Springsteen and Obama, coinciding with the release of* Renegades: Born in the USA *in October 2021.*

2021 ended with an important symbolic event: Springsteen sold his entire catalog (recordings and masters) to Sony for $500 million. He no longer owns his own music. He wasn't the only musician to do so, and in fact he was just the latest in a long series of stars who cashed in on their repertoire. But he was the one to get paid the most (Bob Dylan sold it all for about $400 million, Genesis got around $300 million). The big labels are interested in music catalogs because it's an investment with big earnings that don't fluctuate according to market whims or political decisions. Instead, artist catalogs provide a constant, guaranteed inflow of money. For the musicians in that historic moment, on the other hand, a convenient exchange between future royalties and lump-sum cash was a great financial benefit.

It isn't the most noble motivation on the planet, but for a musician who deeply identifies with what he does and who he is, who took decades to make peace with a part of his own catalog, who changed his musical style multiple times and who, only in the later part of his life, found an accord with his origins and accepted a long and varied repertoire in its entirety, setting it free and no longer owning the rights is perhaps the closest thing to a foreshadowing of death.

But giving up isn't his style. And with concerts starting up again, the E Street Band was on the road again for a new round of concerts starting in February 2023.

In 2021, for the record-breaking sum of $500 million, Springsteen sold his entire catalog to Sony.

The world has changed, and music has changed too, in surprising and drastic ways. When Springsteen started out, there were electric guitars and wooden planks as a stage. Today there are plug-ins and the metaverse. But even if everything has changed, for Springsteen, for us, for everyone, what he said at South by Southwest in Austin in 2012 still rings true: "I'd like to talk about one thing that's been consistent over the years. . . .Whether you're making dance music, Americana, rap music, electronica, it's all about how you are putting what you do together. The elements you're using don't matter. Purity of human expression and experience is not confined to guitars, to tubes, to turntables, to microchips. There is no right way, no pure way, of doing it. There's just doing it. We live in a post-authentic world . . . at the end of the day, it's the power and purpose of your music that still matters."

182 *A moment from Springsteen's big return to the stage after the pandemic, on June 26, 2021, with Springsteen on Broadway at the St. James Theatre in New York City.*

SPRINGSTEEN IS "BORN TO RUN," AND WE'LL KEEP RUNNING WITH HIM.

184 and 185 *Two "classic" moments from Springsteen's show: a woman from the crowd got on stage during "Dancing in the Dark," like in the video for the song directed by Brian De Palma.*

186-187 *A scene from the concert Springsteen and the E Street Band played at Capannelle in Rome, July 7, 2013.*

188-189 *The Boss on stage during the Rock in Rio music festival, in Rio de Janeiro, 2013.*

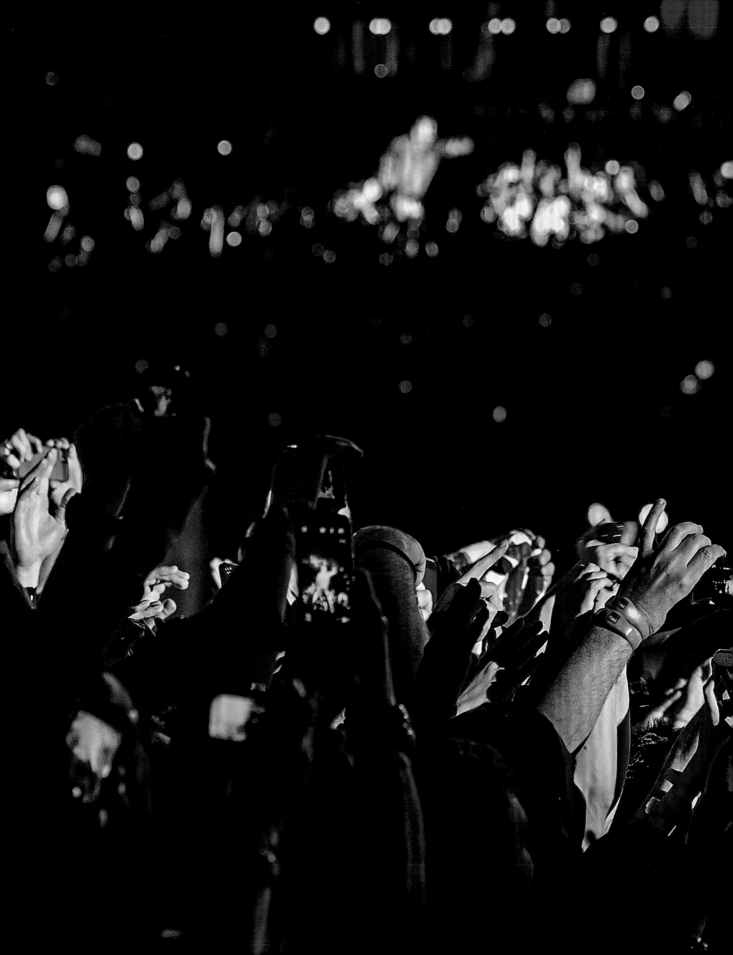

190-191 *Drummer Max Weinberg accompanies* *Little Steven, Springsteen, and Patti Scialfa* *during* The River *tour in Washington, DC.*

192 and 193 *Two moments from Springsteen's show at the Oracle Arena in Oakland, California, on March 13, 2016.*

194-195 *Springsteen on stage in Rock in Rio Lisboa, in the Portuguese capital, 2016.*

196-197 *Springsteen and the E Street Band playing at San Siro Stadium in Milan, July 2016.*

198-199 *Springsteen during a concert in Paris, 2016.*

200-201, 202, 202-203, and 204-205 *Springsteen on stage and backstage during Stand Up for Heroes at Madison Square Garden, New York City, November 2019, an annual fundraising event for war veterans.*

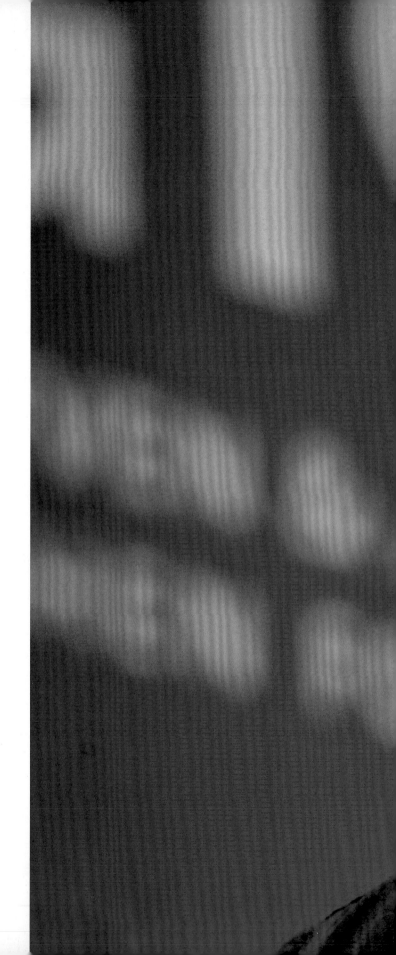

"ALL THAT I'VE FOUND
TRUE AND I SENT IT IN
MY LETTER TO YOU."

THE AUTHOR

ERNESTO ASSANTE began working in journalism in 1977. In his forty-plus-year career, he has collaborated with numerous weekly and monthly Italian and international publications, including *Epoca, L'Espresso,* and *Rolling Stone.* He conceived of and oversaw the "Music," "Computer Valley," and "Computer, Internet and More" supplements for *la Repubblica.* He is the author of books on music criticism, a few of which were co-written with his colleague Gino Castaldo. In 2005, the two created "Lezioni di Rock. Viaggio al Centro della Musica" (Lessons in Rock. A Voyage into the Heart of Music). From 2003 to 2009, he taught New Media Theory and Technique, followed by Analysis of Musical Styles, at La Sapienza University in Rome as part of the Communication Sciences curricula. He currently teaches the History of Popular Music at the Milan Conservatory. For White Star, he has written multiple books on music that have been published all around the world.

The author would like to extend a special thank-you to Gabriele Niola, whose invaluable research made this book possible.

Photo Credits

Project editor

Valeria Manferto De Fabianis

Graphic design

Paola Piacco

whitestar°

WS whitestar™ is a trademark property of White Star s.r.l.

© 2023 White Star s.r.l.
Piazzale Luigi Cadorna, 6
20123 Milan, Italy
www.whitestar.it

Translator: Katherine Kirby
Editor: Phillip Gaskill

ISBN 978-88-544-2034-2
2 3 4 5 6   28 27 26 25 24

Printed in China